Today for Tomorrow

A Field Guide to Strategic Foresight

Maggie Kolkena

Jeana Kats

Today for Tomorrow / Maggie Kolkena and Jeana Kats—2nd ed.

Paperback ISBN 978-1-956989-14-4

Contents

Foreword

In our leadership development work, my colleagues and I have noticed the signs of a turning tide. The responsibility for cultivating strategic foresight is no longer considered the sole purview of external experts or specialized teams. A pivotal shift is underway: leaders across the organization—from the boardroom to the front lines—are stepping in to help chart the course of the future.

This shift isn't hypothetical—it's the natural next step in leadership evolution. We've seen it before. Early on, skills like strategy, team development and coaching were the domain of external specialists. Organizations retained an external strategy expert, team development facilitator or executive coach. Over time, these capabilities became the expectation of every leader.

In the 1980s, organizations relied heavily on external consultants—me included—to formulate strategic plans. Over the following two decades, strategic thinking transitioned from a specialized capability into a foundational leadership skill, taught and expected of managers at all levels. Similarly, team development and executive coaching emerged in the 1990s as specialized services provided by boutique firms. Today, every leader is expected to be able to coach and develop others.

I believe that strategic foresight is following a familiar path—from niche expertise to widespread leadership expectation.

This evolution began in the early 2000s. While working with senior teams at Fortune 500 companies, my colleagues and I noticed that CEOs were voicing concerns about "long-term disruption." Models like the *Three Horizons of Growth* urged leaders to look past the short term—but in truth they didn't know how.

We responded by bringing in futurists—hybrid professionals equal parts economist, social scientist, and storyteller. They would join leadership offsites, offer forecasts for the next five years, share likely disruptions…and leave. What they provided was compelling—but

> The real problem of humanity is the following: we have paleolithic emotions; medieval institutions; and god-like technology.
>
> E.O. WILSON, AMERICAN BIOLOGIST AND NATURALIST

too often, it stayed in the realm of interesting conversation, not meaningful action.

Why? Because external experts often lack what we call "stickiness": the ability to translate ideas into context-specific, actionable change.

Fast forward twenty years, and organizations that are early adopters are taking bold steps to internalize strategic foresight:

- Establishing strategic insight teams that report directly to senior leadership
- Recruiting from institutions that formally teach foresight and insight
- Building disciplined planning processes that include regular reviews of long-term disruptions and responses

This evolution is underway. Many organizations now have strategic foresight functions or centers of excellence—and, as mentioned at the outset, we're on the brink of the next shift: making strategic foresight a skill all leaders possess.

That's where Maggie and Jeana's work shines.

They bring three vital strengths to the table:

1. Expertise in imparting strategic foresight—not just possessing it. They've distilled complex models into accessible frameworks that leaders can use.
2. Masterful learning facilitation—the rhythm and structure of their book reflect deep knowledge of how adults learn.
3. A proven commitment to application—this is about equipping leaders to act, not just theorize.

In spirit, this book belongs on the same shelf as *Competitive Strategy* by Michael Porter, *The One Minute Manager* by Ken Blanchard, *The GROW Model* by John Whitmore and *The Five Dysfunctions of a Team* by Patrick Lencioni—all pivotal texts that democratized essential leadership skills.

Today for Tomorrow gives leaders the tools to develop strategic foresight independently. That alone makes it worth your time. It can change the way you think, and, in my experience, this is what distinguishes the most effective leaders – the willingness to immerse themselves in the next source of complexity and letting it drive your growth.

I wish you well on your journey.

Susan P. Dunn, PhD.

Prologue

It was June 2020 and approximately sixty of us from around the world were gathered online to launch a Strategic Foresight Series for the strategic planners of a large tech company division. We're all on camera, except the team members in Taiwan—it's past their bedtime and they're in their PJs. The sponsoring executive welcomes everyone and begins with these three words: *"Everything is different. Everything is different."* All nodded in stunned agreement.

Indeed, nearly everything had to change. The way we worked in the past was no longer possible as the 2020 global pandemic worsened. Every organization was impacted in some way. Telemedicine exploded as restrictions were enacted and patients adapted. Restaurants built their delivery and takeout capabilities. Buses were outfitted with barriers, reconfigured seating, and air filtration systems. Zoom became the new meeting place, and our homes were reorganized to accommodate virtual offices, home gyms, and classrooms.

We are a resilient species in a crisis. But does it have to take a calamity to spur needed adaptation? Moreover, can we see the need to adapt in advance and prepare for the future now? How can we anticipate the next big change before it arrives—and be ready for it, maybe even thrive in it? Is that possible?

THE MOVE FROM VUCA TO BANI

The shift from VUCA to BANI marks an evolution in how we make sense of a rapidly changing world. VUCA—standing for Volatile, Uncertain, Complex, and Ambiguous—was coined by the U.S. Army in the late 1980s to describe the unpredictable, post-Cold War environment and was later adopted by businesses to navigate globalization and technological disruption. However, as crises became more frequent and destabilizing—such as climate shocks, pandemics, and social unrest—VUCA no longer fully captured the intensity of modern challenges. In response, futurist Jamais Cascio introduced BANI: Brittle, Anxious, Nonlinear, and Incomprehensible. BANI reflects not just change, but breakdown—where systems can shatter, fear drives decisions, and cause and effect are obscured.

Welcome

Welcome to the world of strategic foresight. We're excited to share a methodology and set of tools that will help you plan for uncertainty and generate value-creating growth.

We wrote this book for people who want to utilize strategic foresight to make their organization more resilient, more prepared for the future, and more equipped to make future-related decisions. There are many methods of strategic foresight. This book offers an introduction to a classic strategic foresight methodology. It is well suited to the leader or facilitator who wants to begin strategic foresight work and is looking for a practical and organized approach to guide the process.

Maggie, the co-author of this book, had the good fortune of being introduced to strategic foresight tools in the early 2000s when she was the organization development manager for Intel Labs. She learned the strategic foresight process through the Global Business Network, experts and leaders in the field at the time. Jeana, the second co-author of this book, was the HR Business Partner for Intel Labs, experiencing the process for the first time. Since then, we have helped hundreds of leaders learn how to do strategic foresight work. Along the way, we discovered what was helpful in learning the process and made improvements. The result is a proven set of steps that leaders like you can successfully use on their own. That's the key goal of this book: to make you self-sufficient. The first time out, you'll be functional but not an expert. We encourage you to summon the courage to be imperfect in the beginning.

"How do you take strategic action when the future is uncertain and changing quickly?"

Today for Tomorrow

Several years ago, Maggie had the pleasure of coaching David, a tech executive. Like any senior exec, he had a lot of responsibilities and demands on his time. During one coaching session, he shared his guide for allocating his time. He did what he needed to do to manage the current quarter and fiscal year and called that "Today for Today." But David also had a discipline around preparing his organization for the future. He called it "Today for Tomorrow." We love this simple description—which he modestly assured us he hadn't invented—and the phrase has stayed with us. Foresight work is one way to act Today for Tomorrow.

A spark ignited the flame during a series of coaching calls where we heard the same refrain. One leader summed it up, "Okay, I get it—planning for the long-term is important. But what do I do—just think big thoughts?" The purpose of this book is to provide a scope and process for "thinking big thoughts" to prepare for tomorrow.

We have combined our coaching, leadership development, and strategic foresight expertise to create a strategic foresight approach that broadly fits the needs of leaders. We've worked with strategic foresight now for over twenty years, and since 2018 have been creating experiences to help leaders grow this skill. It's been gratifying to see the uptake. Foresight work has never been more relevant.

This book is for all leaders who want to prepare their organizations for the future.

Using This Book

Strategic foresight is an art and a science; it requires use of both the right and left side of your brain. You'll have the science—the toolkit as well as data such as demographics, climate models, and technological forecasts. The art lies in how you facilitate the process, the judgment around what good looks like, how much data is enough, and other qualitative judgments that make the tools sing. This comes with practice. Whether your organization is a small business, a not-for-profit, a business unit, or a multinational corporation, the tools will work for you. And, happily, research suggests that creating and using scenarios gets easier and faster with practice (Ramirez, Bhatti and Tapinos, 2020).

We have broken the full strategic foresight process into ten stages; each chapter covers a stage. In each chapter, you'll find:

- A step-by-step description detailing how to create the outcome of each stage
- Sidebars with extra information or client stories
- Lots of examples
- A QR code to take you to the latest resources as well as fresh stories
- Your Turn: a section to practice what you've just read

Along the way, we'll share our best tips and techniques.

We're glad you're here.

Part One

An Introduction to
Strategic Foresight

Historical Development of Strategic Foresight

Most researchers would agree that the emergence of the foresight discipline has two roots.

The U.S. military, with help from RAND Corporation's Herman Kahn, initially used scenarios in the 1950s for military strategy and possible outcomes of nuclear conflict challenges during the Cold War. Kahn pioneered the use of rigorous, expert-driven approaches to futures analysis, establishing foresight as a technical discipline requiring specialized knowledge and analytical skills. If this intrigues you, check out Kahn's book called "On Thermonuclear War" (Kahn, 1960).

Gaston Berger is viewed as the second founder of strategic foresight. He founded "la prospective" as a philosophical discipline, establishing the core principle that the future is not predetermined but can be actively shaped through human intention and action. In contrast to Kahn's work, Gaston developed participatory, collaborative methodologies that democratized future thinking beyond expert analysts, making strategic foresight accessible to broader groups of stakeholders (Rohrbeck, Battistell, and Huizingh, 2015).

Strategic foresight found its way to the business world when planners from the Royal Dutch Shell anticipated the 1970s oil embargo. Shell created a scenario in which oil-producing countries (OPEC) would either dramatically raise prices or cut supply. When the 1973 oil crisis hit and oil prices quadrupled, Shell was one of the only major oil companies prepared (Hines, 2013).

The 1980s and 1990s marked a turning point for strategic foresight work. To stay competitive, firms integrated and extended foresight processes beyond informing decision-making to play an increased role in strategy development and innovation. Daimler and Deutsche Bank are two corporations that established think tanks during this period.

One of the most renowned examples of strategic foresight occurred in the early 1990s, where a team of economists, activists, and policymakers embarked on what they called the "Mont Fleur scenario exercise" to imagine South Africa's transition from apartheid to democracy (le Roux, 1992). Through the creation of four scenarios, participants were better equipped to find common ground and to understand the consequences of different political and economic choices. This contributed to more informed decision-making during the transition period. (You will learn more about Mont Fleur later in this book).

From the 2000s to the present, strategic foresight continues to gain momentum though not without bumps. It can be difficult to quantify strategic foresight's role in value contribution (Marinkovic, Al-Tabba, Khan, and Wu, 2022). Firms also struggle with fostering a "foresight" culture. And some strategic foresight processes and tools are better than others. That is where this book comes in.

What Is Strategic Foresight?

Strategic foresight is a structured process that looks at future possibilities—beyond the official or desired future. It picks up where traditional strategic planning leaves off. It does not replace it.

At the heart of the process are "scenarios," stories that portray how potential futures may evolve. These stories bring the possible futures to life and allow us to address the future's risks and opportunities in today's strategic plans.

However, the purpose of strategic foresight work goes beyond creating scenarios. The purpose of strategic foresight work is to:

- Change mental models as you prepare for the future
- Stress test your current strategy
- Identify proactive steps on future opportunities such as new markets, products, and other innovative plays
- Take defensive action on future vulnerabilities and risks

It is a flexible, intuitive framework and can be easily tailored to fit your unique needs.

What Are the Outcomes of Strategic Foresight?

The concrete outcomes are the set of possible futures to analyze and the strategic options you'll generate. But the process delivers more.

In our chapter on "Why Strategic Foresight", we talk about reasons why organizational growth is so difficult. Strategic foresight can help address many of those challenges. Here's what we've observed as leaders have learned how to do strategic foresight work.

> "Think of scenarios as different hands of cards you might be dealt; think of strategies as the way you would play those cards."
>
> JAY OGILVY, COFOUNDER OF GLOBAL BUSINESS NETWORK

Expanded Mindset

Sometimes the very expertise for which we are valued gets in our way. We can fall victim to biased thinking when we become an expert and then fail to perceive what doesn't fit into our expertise. In the first steps of strategic foresight, you'll gather data around forces that are impacting the world in which you do business. You will be looking at trends in many fields and dive deep into some of them. You'll become aware of how much information about the future is available and how little we see in a typical day. Your day-to-day aperture will open, and you'll become aware of things going on around you—beyond short-term fire drills. Strategic foresight will open your "future aperture."

Greater Ability to Navigate Ambiguity

The future IS uncertain and yet a key outcome of strategic foresight is removing the risk that a future disruption will surprise you and compromise your ability to respond. Rather than triggering the brain's stress response to uncertainty, scenario work transforms ambiguity from a threat into a strategic asset. By explicitly mapping multiple possibilities, we satisfy our brain's need for structure while maintaining the flexibility required for adaptive strategy.

A New Thinking Framework

Once you become familiar with creating a scenario grid, you can use it as a thinking tool. Very quickly, you can parse a complex problem and organize your thinking around it. Strategic foresight provides an organizing framework and logic for thinking about the future of multi-faceted issues.

Better Team Discussions

Groupthink is a natural consequence for teams, especially when there are no perfect answers. The strategic foresight process is structured and agnostic. You'll test whether your ideas will meet future needs. The process also ensures that you are thorough in your thinking and have considered many alternatives. Are you challenging one another's thinking? Have you questioned conventional wisdom? Are sacred cows limiting options? Strategic foresight can help expand the capacity to open these conversations and structure them.

Enhanced Organizational Learning

Strategic foresight builds institutional capability to continuously

> "Scenarios address the collective impact of multiple uncertainties."
>
> PAUL SCHOEMAKER, FOUNDING PRESIDENT OF SOCIAL VENTURE PARTNERS INTERNATIONAL

"I still think that business can be the greatest agent for positive change in the world. We have to dream a different dream. We have to have an aspirational vision of the future. I believe that that's possible."

ROSE MARCARIO,
FORMER CEO
PATAGONIA

scan, sense, and adapt rather than just react to disruption. Organizations develop "future fitness"—muscle memory to regularly question assumptions, test mental models against emerging realities, and update strategies before crisis forces change. This creates a learning organization that treats uncertainty as information rather than threat, systematically building knowledge about how change happens and developing the reflexes to spot weak signals before they become overwhelming trends.

Strategic Foresight for Inspiration

We have a final thought on possible outcomes of strategic foresight work. Projects emerging from strategic foresight often adopt a predominantly reactive, defensive posture—preparing for the next crisis to avoid another emergency. While anticipating and preparing for crises is important, scenarios can also be used to envision and influence more positive futures.

One of the most inspirational examples comes from South Africa's post-apartheid transition. In the early 1990s, many factions held strong and diverse positions about the country's future. Twenty-two representatives from recently legalized parties came together to explore the decade ahead through an exercise called the Mont Fleur Scenarios (le Roux, 1992). The name was intentionally chosen to indicate that the scenarios belonged to the group that met at Mont Fleur, not to any specific institution, party, or organization. Members participated in their personal capacities.

Together, they created four vivid and plausible futures. One scenario—"Flight of the Flamingos"—served as inspiration for a shared vision of a possible future in which everyone rises slowly, but together. A report describing the scenarios was distributed as an insert in a national newspaper, and a video was created. The team then presented and discussed the scenarios with more than fifty groups, including political parties, companies, academics, trade unions, and civic organizations.

The simple message of the Flight of the Flamingos scenario conveyed a belief in the potential for a positive outcome. In a country amid turbulence and uncertainty, a credible and optimistic story made a strong impact. As one participant reflected, "We mapped out in very broad terms the outline of a successful outcome, which is now being filled in. We captured the way forward of those committed to finding a way forward" (Kahane, 2004).

Why Strategic Foresight?

The Growth Challenge

Very few companies manage to sustain long-term growth. Over the past eight decades, the average lifespan of a US S&P 500 company has dropped from 67 to 15 years. The research also shows a typical company grew just 2.8% per year during the ten years preceding COVID-19, and only one in eight recorded more than 10% annual growth (McKinsey & Company, Corporate Performance Analytics).

Why do companies flounder with long-term growth?

AVERAGE COMPANY LIFESPAN PROJECTION

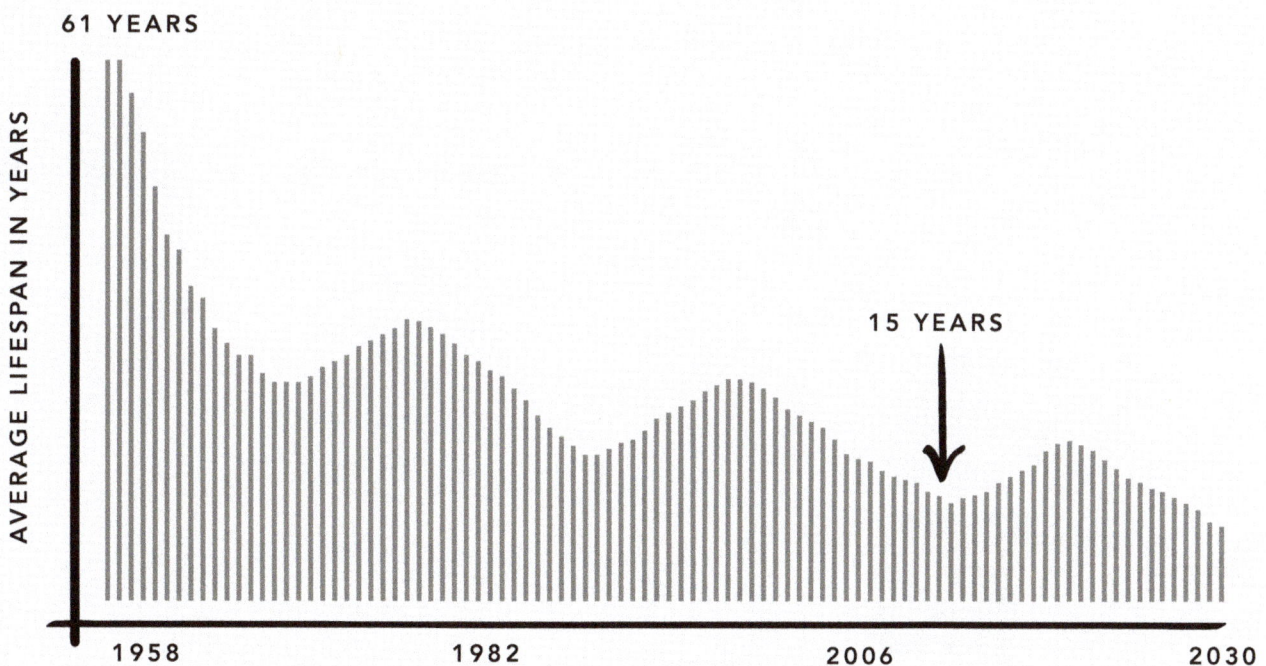

61 YEARS

AVERAGE LIFESPAN IN YEARS

15 YEARS

1958   1982   2006   2030

The Tyranny of the Short-Term

For numerous decades, Maggie and Jeana have coached leaders who have told us they continue to receive the following feedback: "Be more strategic." We often anonymously poll leaders in workshops, asking them to indicate where they spend most of their time. It varies, of course, but even at senior leadership levels, we've estimated that leaders spend 50-90% of their time on the short-term and just 5-10% on the long-term.

It's not surprising. Most organizations have a bias for the short-term. Publicly traded companies, in particular, are dependent on equity markets that place greater value on fiscal targets and short-term (read: quarterly) results. These companies are fungible to investors. Investors rarely have allegiances to the companies they invest in. Executive compensation structures reinforce this, incentivizing short-term wins over long-term investments in growth.

Why do leaders stay involved in the short-term? Here is what they say:

"I don't mind having my hand in the game."
"My company recognizes and rewards based on my accomplishments in the current year."
"I can solve problems faster because I've been around the block more times."
"This is the part of the work I like."

There are many other internal and external reasons that come into play. Let's look at a few more.

Internal Challenges

- Paradox of Growth: Growth, particularly rapid growth, introduces complexity, which can, in turn, hinder future growth and profitability. For example, when revenue increases faster than the company's ability to hire and manage talent, this can create an internal imbalance.
- Founder's Mentality Erosion: As companies scale, they can lose the agility, customer focus, and commitment to a clear mission that characterized their early success.
- Bureaucracy and Rigidity: Larger organizations are more susceptible to becoming bureaucratic and rigid, which can slow down decision-making, stifle innovation, and lead to a lack of agility.
- Complexity and Lack of Focus: As companies grow, they may struggle to maintain clarity and direction, leading to scope creep and a lack of strategic discipline.
- Inability to Mobilize Resources: Growth can put a strain on resources, making it difficult to allocate resources effectively, pursue new opportunities, or address challenges quickly and effectively.

THE THREE HORIZONS OF GROWTH

Need evidence? McKinsey & Company interviewed organizations with strong growth histories and others who had underperformed their peers (Baghai, Coley, and White, 1999). When they compared leadership practices, they found that one practice that distinguished the growth leaders from the underperformers was that high growth leaders attended to three distinct time horizons: H1 – near-term, H2 – mid-term, and H3 – long-term. Underperformers focused on just the near-term and mid-term. In the most successful organizations, leaders focused efforts on all three horizons.

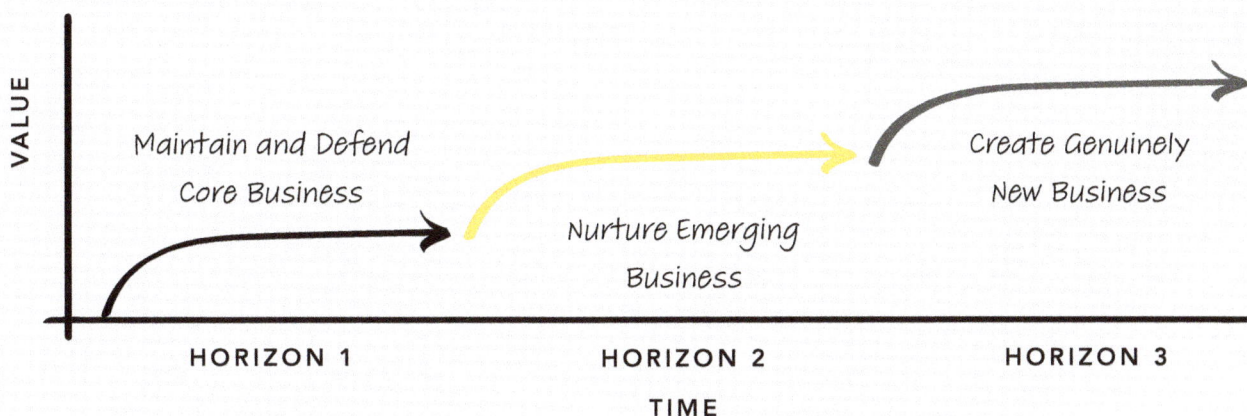

VALUE

Maintain and Defend
Core Business

Nurture Emerging
Business

Create Genuinely
New Business

HORIZON 1   **HORIZON 2**   **HORIZON 3**

TIME

- Inadequate Strategic Planning: Poor planning and lack of a clear strategy for long-term growth can lead to stagnation or even failure.
- Resistance to Change: Businesses that fail to adapt to evolving market conditions, new technologies, or shifts in customer preferences risk becoming obsolete.
- Financial Mismanagement: Ineffective cash flow management, undercapitalization, and unsustainable growth can severely impact a company's ability to maintain operations and invest in future growth initiatives.

External Challenges

> "Concurrent shocks, deeply interconnected risks and eroding resilience are giving rise to the risk of polycrises — where disparate crises interact such that the overall impact far exceeds the sum of each part."
>
> WORLD ECONOMIC FORUM'S GLOBAL RISKS REPORT, 2023

- Increased Competition: As a company grows and gains market share, it inevitably faces heightened competition. This can force businesses to lower prices, reduce profit margins, and invest more in marketing, ultimately trapping themselves in a competitive spiral.
- Market Dynamics and Customer Needs: The market can shift rapidly due to new technologies, changing consumer behavior, or unforeseen events. Companies must be agile and responsive to these shifts to avoid being left behind.
- Economic Uncertainty: Economic fluctuations, such as inflation, interest rate changes, and supply chain disruptions, can create an unstable environment, impacting profitability and growth potential.
- Political and Geopolitical Uncertainty: Political instability and geopolitical conflicts can disrupt markets and affect regulations, taxation, and trade policies, generating an unpredictable environment.

The Limits of Traditional Planning

Imagine there are multiple, possible futures for your organization.

The first future can be called the Official Future—the one contained in your strategic plans. The diagram below covers approximately two to five years. At that point, there is likely some variance (10%) in what the future might hold. But that variance is narrow enough that the organization can lock into the plan and tolerate the variance. Strategic models are leveraged to help create this strategy, and most organizations have protocols to facilitate this process.

But what happens to the organization if, in five to ten years' time, the future strays outside the 10% variance? Our world is moving too fast and is too complex for standard planning tools. In this case, a different type of planning is required—one that holds multiple possible futures. This is where a strategic foresight methodology is needed.

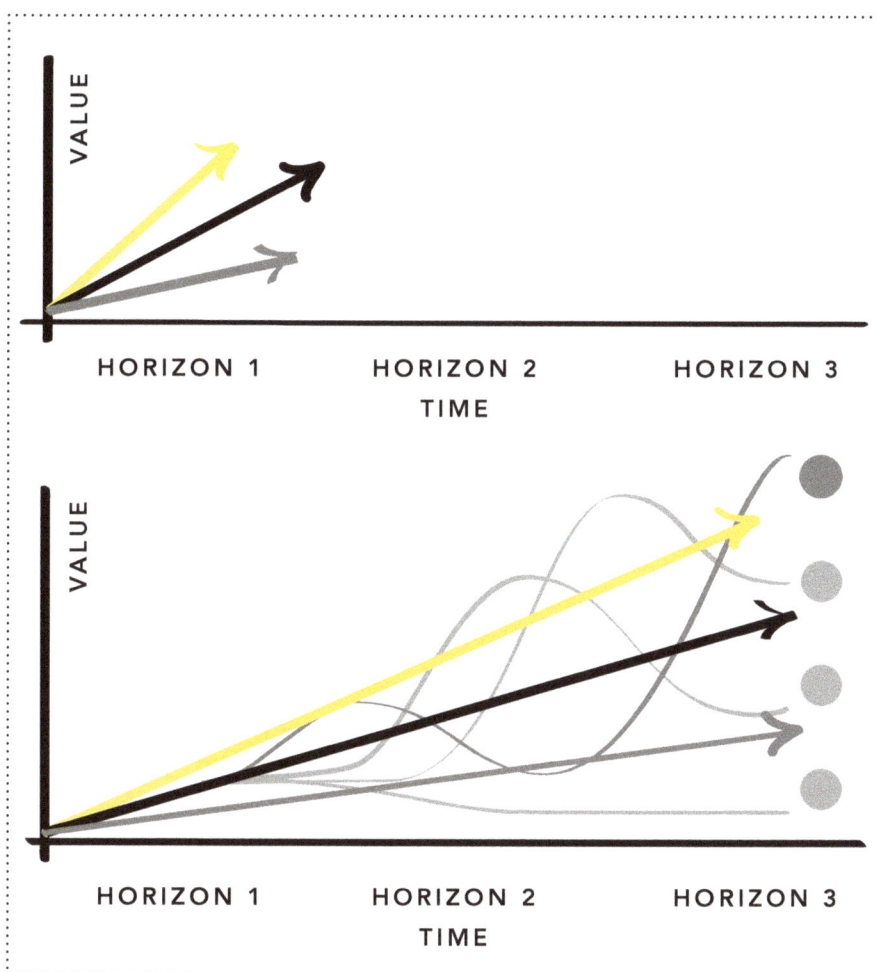

> "We think, each of us, that we're much more rational than we are."
>
> DANIEL KAHNEMAN, ISRAELI-AMERICAN PSYCHOLOGIST

Uncertainty increases as you go forward in time

How To Do Strategic Foresight

How Does Strategic Foresight Work?

Strategic foresight consists of multiple steps or stages. The process begins by defining your focus and gathering data that indicates what the future might hold. This information is used to generate pictures of various futures that could unfold. By analyzing the multiple possibilities inherent in the possible futures, you will identify some strategic moves that will prepare your organization to thrive in the future.

The Strategic Foresight Process

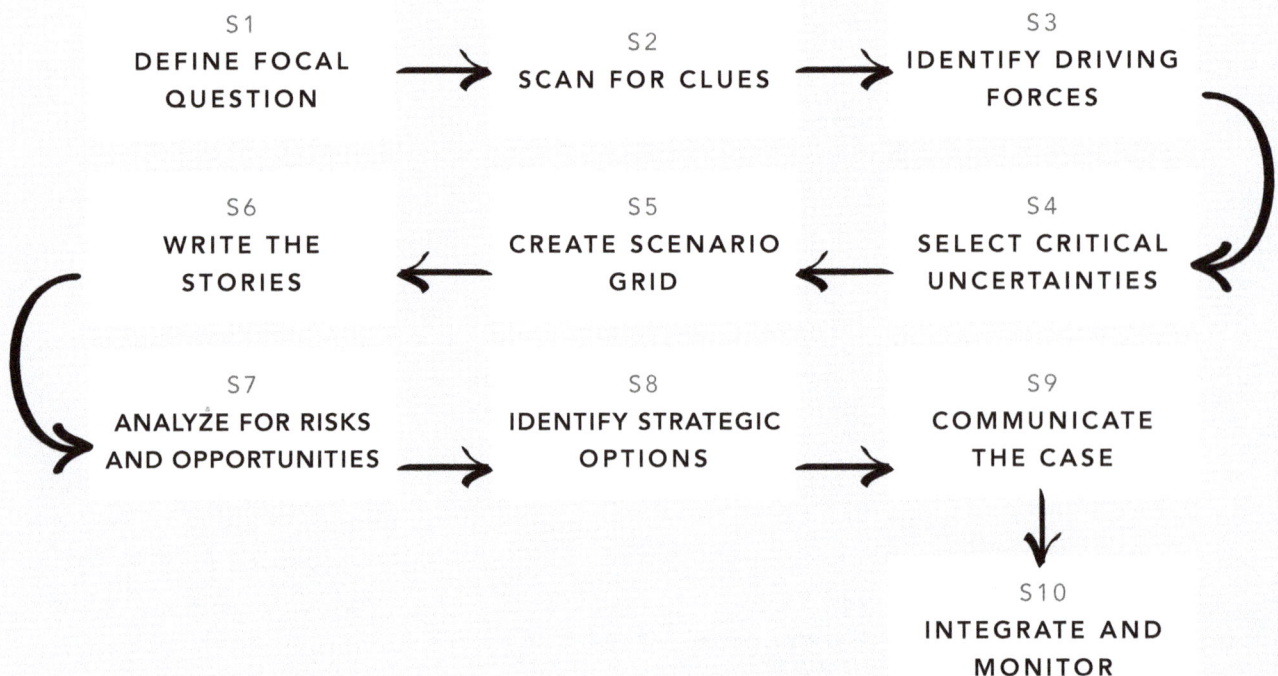

S1	S2	S3
DEFINE FOCAL QUESTION	SCAN FOR CLUES	IDENTIFY DRIVING FORCES

S6	S5	S4
WRITE THE STORIES	CREATE SCENARIO GRID	SELECT CRITICAL UNCERTAINTIES

S7	S8	S9
ANALYZE FOR RISKS AND OPPORTUNITIES	IDENTIFY STRATEGIC OPTIONS	COMMUNICATE THE CASE

S10
INTEGRATE AND MONITOR

You may have seen the process described with fewer, more complex steps. We've chosen to describe the work in ten separate, simple stages which we believe makes our model easy to understand and modular, as sometimes leaders need to use all ten stages and sometimes they need to work through only a few of the stages.

Strategic foresight builds broad awareness of what is going on in the world around you and draws on a wide range of disciplines and interests, including economics, psychology, politics, and technology. It involves both creative and rational thinking. You will evaluate data and use your imagination to generate possibilities. You will develop questions and answers to anticipate the future.

CREATIVE/ART	RATIONAL/SCIENCE
Subjective	Objective
Diverge	Converge
Process	Outcome
Imagination	Data
Vision	Toolkit

Scenario Work is Both an Art and a Science

Throughout the process, you will diverge to generate lots of options and converge to reduce the number of options.

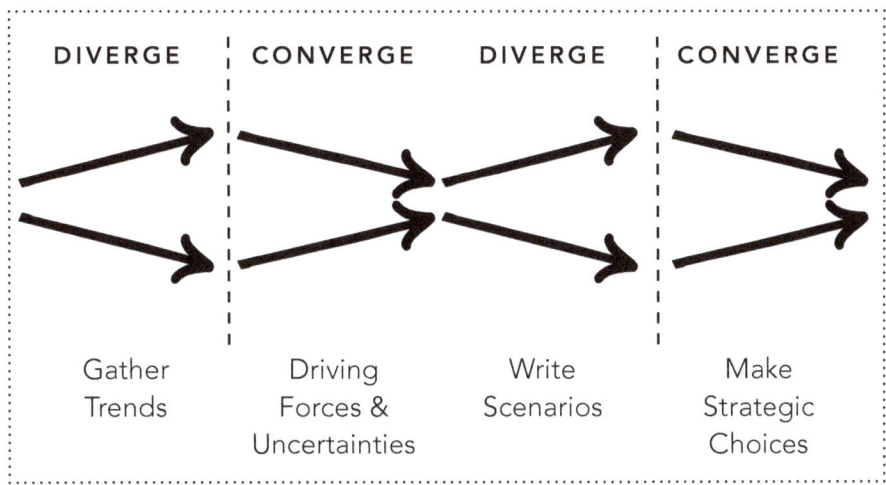

Generating Options and Making Decisions

DIVERGE	CONVERGE	DIVERGE	CONVERGE
Gather Trends	Driving Forces & Uncertainties	Write Scenarios	Make Strategic Choices

Is Strategic Foresight Right for You?

As much as we love strategic foresight work, it is not the answer to every challenge. Here's a decision tree to consider if it's right for you and your organization.

Strategic Foresight Decision Tree

What type of challenge do you want to address — *Clear problems and solutions* → **Strategic foresight is more than you need**

↓

How much uncertainty surrounds the issue — *Low uncertainty* → **Traditional planning will work**

↓

Is your organization open to solutions that challenge current strategy — *No* → **Strategic foresight could require changes to current plan**

↓

Can you gather fellow travellers and resources — *No* → **Too bad...strategic foresight is not a solo sport**

↓

GO FOR IT!

Adapted from WHAT IF? The Art of Scenario Thinking for Nonprofits (Scearce, Fulton and Community, 2004)

The Flexibility of the Model

Strategic foresight can be adjusted to meet your needs. A strategic foresight project can be a VERY large project, taking several months and requiring a broad set of stakeholders and external expertise to inform major strategic decisions. It can also be a way to orient others to future possibilities or as an individual tool to organize thinking.

How To Use Strategic Foresight

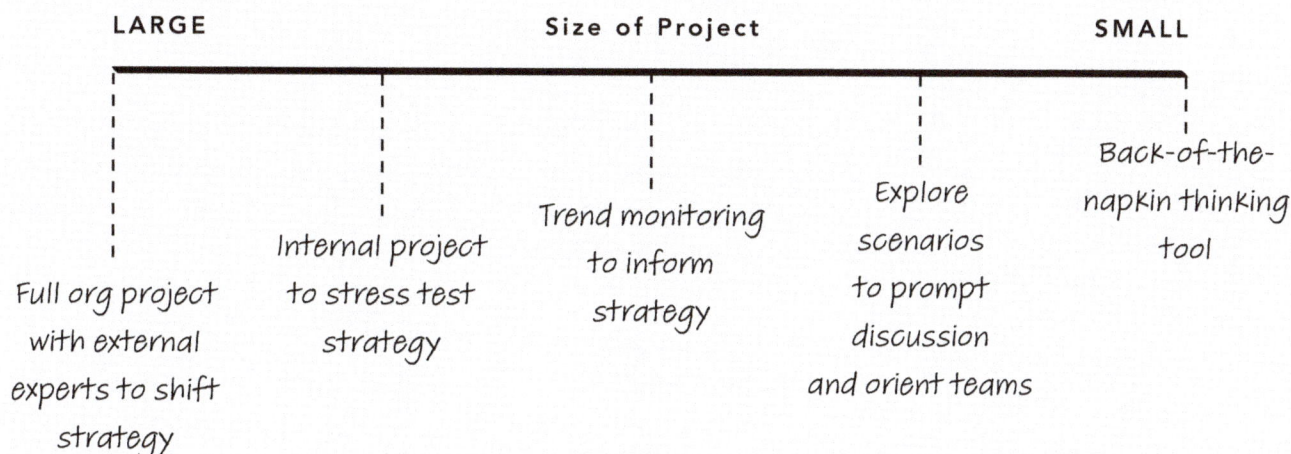

LARGE		Size of Project		SMALL

Full org project with external experts to shift strategy

Internal project to stress test strategy

Trend monitoring to inform strategy

Explore scenarios to prompt discussion and orient teams

Back-of-the-napkin thinking tool

Leaders we've supported have used the entire process or a single step of the process to inform decisions. As you become more familiar with the various stages of the process, you may see many opportunities to use strategic foresight thinking to support business discussions and decision-making.

Who Should Do Strategic Foresight?

No matter where you sit in your organization, if you have a need to answer, "what if", strategic foresight is relevant for you. As an organizational development practitioner, you can bring this to your groups and facilitate the process. If you're in finance or revenue, this has relevance to your work. If you're in sales, this will help prepare your team to meet targets in difficult times. If you're in employee development, this is a competence you can build in the organization. If you're in supply chain or manufacturing, you will discover many insights, both internal and external, to your company.

No matter where you sit in your organization, if you have a need to answer, "what if", strategic foresight is relevant for you.

Finding Fellow Travelers

FORESIGHT IN A MULTINATIONAL

Kim is a senior leader in a Fortune 100 company. She and her colleagues felt the need to deepen their company's ability to generate long-term insights. They had a trend tracking capability but got stuck moving from trends to action. Kim was part of an executive development session we delivered that used strategic foresight work to address a top corporate challenge. She immediately recognized the value of the process. She socialized it with her execs and embedded some of the stages into a strategy session to develop insights for a key consumer segment. The marketing leaders reported that the process allowed them to put better-informed plans in place. Based on this feedback, Kim's role has been expanded to lead a group with the mandate to help all leaders develop strategic foresight skills.

Earlier in this book, we discussed why long-term, Horizon Three thinking is critical for an organization's resilience—if not their survival. We can all think of companies who failed to see important shifts and faltered or failed.

Perhaps you've already been tasked with a scenario project. Or you're planning a strategic foresight project. Maybe you just want to explore strategic foresight work. In any case, this chapter contains some ideas for getting others involved in your strategic foresight work.

The Genius of Teams

Technically, it is possible to conduct strategic foresight work by yourself. But why would you? Working with others means you'll have a broader set of considerations and extra hands. Diversity can help a team avoid groupthink. And the research, whether it's from McKinsey, Gartner, or World Economic Forum - the findings are consistent: Teams with greater diversity have better outcomes.

What do we mean by diversity? You want different perspectives. Strive for diversity in gender, race, upbringing, experience, education, thinking styles—all of these will ensure you have a bigger collective brain.

Strategic foresight work is not intended to be interesting reading material. Sadly, no one is going to be gobsmacked into action by a smart scenario. You need fellow travelers. You need partners who are involved and want to join the game.

Somewhere in your network you have colleagues who are also

concerned about your organization's long-term growth and resilience. You have colleagues who have the inclination to look ahead and imagine future opportunities or future challenges. Finding fellow travelers can begin with a simple question: *"Have you seen this article about (THIS)? I've been reading about (THIS), and I think it has the possibility to impact our organization (THIS) way."* Begin holding intriguing conversations with your colleagues.

Check around your organization. If you're in a larger corporation, it's possible that other folks, especially in groups like market insights, labs, R&D, and strategic planning, have done or are doing some level of strategic foresight work.

Ultimately, having many leaders research and consider the future will help your organization be more resilient in the face of unexpected turbulence.

You can meet for a short conversation. Or put a topic on the agenda of a regular meeting and share insights you've gleaned from doing some research. The discussion will be stronger if you can provide some credible data, along with 1) this threat is a danger to us or 2) we're going to miss a window of opportunity.

Principles for Catalytic Leaders

From the outside looking in, it *seems* like organizations have a healthy interest in the long-term. Annual reports underline the importance of long-term thinking, CEOs pledge commitments to long-term sustainability goals, and organizations clamor to be included in long-term index funds. Despite these aspirations, many leaders are entering yet another planning cycle where the strategic planning template does not have a slide addressing anything beyond the current, authorized two- or three-year plan.

Executives themselves are frustrated. They, too, serve the tyranny of the short-term.

It's beyond the scope of this book to take on the economic structure

INITIATING THE CONVERSATION

When trying to find fellow travelers, we suggest you don't even mention the term "strategic foresight." Most leaders are wary of the next new management fad, and they don't have any extra time to give away. What you need to find is the CONCERN for or INTEREST in doing a better job of managing the future. Start with: "Dang, I wish our organization wasn't so short-term focused." When you hear an "Amen!" then you have an opening to explore further.

> "Never doubt that a small group of thoughtful, committed citizens can change the world; indeed, it's the only thing that ever has."
>
> MARGARET MEAD, AMERICAN CULTURAL ANTHROPOLOGIST, AUTHOR AND SPEAKER

of the world. Yet the goal of this book is to make strategic foresight 'sticky'—ensuring that the tools actually 'stick' and get used.

Leaders play a role in creating energy for change where they are. This is not to say that it's all up to you and that the top leaders of the organization have no role. As mentioned earlier, many CEOs and executive teams have publicly stated their aspirations for the long-term, but they can't change things in the belly of the organization by themselves. It takes catalysts. The fact that you've decided to explore strategic foresight means you might be ready to be a catalyst to create positive change for your organization.

There is evidence that it is completely possible to start with yourself, party of one. Daniel Stillman, author of Good Talk, cites several studies that suggest change can start anywhere with one person (Stillman, 2022).

First, you don't have to win everyone over. Experiments conducted at Annenberg School found that you need about 25% of a group before a critical mass kicks in (Wei, 2018). But one person can initiate things by finding the early adopters and getting them on board. Who are three to five early adopters you can invite? If you gather the right crew, you'll begin to create a critical mass.

The act of invitation is critical. It ensures that people are involved for their own reasons. Choosing the right people means you don't have to cajole. Find others who can motivate themselves and even be a source of encouragement for you.

Finally, you have significant influence with your "operative network"—those with whom you have frequent interactions. This means that your voice can rival and even exceed that of the official culture. By changing your behavior, others will follow—even if it involves taking risks.

You can create energy for strategic foresight work that leads to action. Let's get started!

Part Two

The Ten Stages

S1: Generate a Focal Question

Sit for a moment and reflect on the future of your organization. You know the current state. But what does the future hold? Really. Take a little time to think about it.

Is there a particular issue concerning you? Maybe it's an emerging concern and you're only hearing a little about it now. For instance, maybe you work at a private college, and you wonder if the future of collegiate education will be primarily online with very little (or zero) in-person learning. Will students still get a high-quality education? Should you combine with other schools? Maybe you're in supply chain. The global pandemic exposed the weaknesses of the system, but what's next? Should you reemphasize local channels?

Are you curious about a specific opportunity? Maybe you've learned about a new approach, a new technology, an innovation that's just gaining traction. Let's say you work in the food industry. You've read that robotic technology can cook meat to the perfect temperature—rare, medium, well—no chef required. A few of your competitors are already installing these devices. Should your company do the same? Maybe this is an excellent opportunity. Or maybe your customers will balk at the notion of a meal cooked by a robot.

When imagining the future, hundreds of questions might pop into your head—what if THIS happens? Or THAT? And what about THIS? You can feel energized but also overwhelmed. That's why it's important to select your focus. You can't consider everything. Focus keeps things manageable.

The first step in your strategic foresight work is to create a focal question to guide your exploration. The focal question sets the boundaries. It defines what is in and what is out.

In nature, an ecosystem is a biological community of living creatures that interact and depend on one another. In business, an ecosystem describes the network of interacting and interdependent entities. For instance, Silicon Valley has entities that are connected through universities, research centers, large technology companies, and start-ups. And then there are all the adjacencies: venture capital firms, lawyers, branding companies, accountants, headhunters, and so on.

Your organization's ecosystem probably isn't contained in a single "biome," but you're still connected in your interdependent system.

Start with Your Internal Stakeholders

Your focal question needs to include your key stakeholders' perspectives to ensure relevance. You can start close to your base and work out from there. Talk to the leadership above you, outside your function, and internal customers. Talk to naysayers. Whenever we've initiated a change project, we ask people who openly express discontent and we always learn something important.

What Does Your Ecosystem Think?

Another important part of evolving your focal question is talking with players in your organization's ecosystem. Each stakeholder has a different reality and different opinions. Your project will benefit from multiple points of view.

Who are the key stakeholders in your organization's ecosystem?

- Customers
- Competitors
- Suppliers
- Communities
- Partners
- Distributors
- Regulators

- Investors
- Trade Associations
- Project Teams
- Board of Directors
- Shareholders
- Volunteers

What are their burning issues? What encouraging trends and concerning trends are they seeing? What changes would they like to see? Once you've talked with a representative sample, you should have some good themes to include in your work.

Crafting Your Focal Questions

There are three parts to a focal question:
- The scope
- The category
- The timeframe

For example:

*What **might** the global (scope: who/where) supply chain (category: what) look like in seven years (time: when)?*

The language is intentionally open. Notice the use of *"what MIGHT it look like"* in the future. You're not predicting a single correct answer. You're imagining multiple possibilities. *"How WILL (THIS) look in seven years?"* This signals to your brain that you're looking for one answer and striving for a prediction. But strategic foresight work is not about making predictions. *"How MIGHT (THIS) look in seven years?"* tells your brain to relax and entertain multiple options.

Here are a few more examples:

What might the U.S. coastal community experience be in ten years?

How might global AI talent be managed in ten years?

What might elementary education for countries with shrinking populations look like in ten years?

These are all examples of focal questions that include scope, category, and timeframe.

Let's look more closely at the three parts.

The Scope
Scope means the extent of the area or subject matter you're dealing with. Are you looking at real estate transactions in California or the entire United States? Commercial real estate or residential? These are very different scopes. Are you investigating the future of tourism in Hawaii or tourism globally? Again, two different scopes. All Amazon customers or just those over the age of sixty-five? Scope describes where you will look and who might be involved.

*What might the future of **low-lying coastal communities** be in ten years?*

*How might **western states** manage water shortages in ten years?*

*How might the **Alpha Generation** affect visual learning methods in five years?*

How will you decide your scope? As we know from the 2020 global pandemic and the persistent supply chain issues, very few of us are unaffected by events in other parts of the world. If you are working for a local organization, you may choose to create your scope more locally. On the other hand, if you have customers beyond your geographic area, you may want to expand your scope. Also, consider trends that began in Asia, Africa, Europe, or South America that might have value for you. Even if you are taking a regional scope, you will likely want to scan globally when you get to Stage 2.

The Category

Category means whatever kind of activity you're exploring to inform your strategic foresight process. For instance, home improvement, online gaming, and leisure travel.

*What might **home improvement** look like in the U.S. in eight years?*

*How might **online gaming** look in ten years?*

*What might the future of **family leisure travel** be in ten years?*

Products or services could be a category:

- Fast food
- Clothing
- Utilities
- Cars
- Toys
- Electronics
- Event management
- Healthcare
- Delivery services
- IT management
- Personal care
- Financial services

*How might **residential utilities** in California be provided in ten years?*

*How might **fast food** be augmented in ten years?*

Professions include functions and fields, like:

- Legal
- Human resources
- Supply chain
- R&D
- Finance
- Operations
- Manufacturing
- Marketing
- Teaching
- Plumbing
- Medicine
- Transportation

*How might **global circular manufacturing for clothing** take place in ten years?*

*How might **decentralized R&D for cyber security** be managed in seven years?*

*What might the future of **marketing for geriatric medicine** be in ten years?*

The Timeframe

This is simply the year for which you'll create your scenarios. As you consider preparing your organization or team for what might lie ahead, you may be asking, "How far out is sufficient? Is two years enough? Should we be looking out ten years?" It depends on a number of considerations. Horizon Three will be different for you based on the pace of change, your industry, and function.

There is no formula to calculate the time frame for you. In our experience, we recommend going out at least five years. Anything less than that makes it difficult to create vivid scenarios that feel different from the current year. Use your judgement. As Jack Sparrow might equivocate, "...it's more what you'd call guidelines than actual rules." The important thing is that you get beyond your short-term frame of mind.

Client Story: Selecting a Focal Question

In 2021, a Fortune 100 technology company asked Maggie to deliver a series of strategic foresight workshops for their entire planning function of over fifty people. The core team (their Chief of Staff (COS) and their HR Business Partner (HRBP) initiated the project. We began by determining the number of teams and generating a unique focal question for each team. This was the series of conversations:

- The core team brainstormed approximately twenty questions.
- The COS and HRBP attended their regular staff meeting and polled the senior team (which included an executive sponsor who reported to the CEO) for their top issues.
- The COS and HRBP brainstormed senior team input and created multiple options for focal questions.
- The core team cleaned up the list, and the COS and HRBP took it back to the senior team for final selection.
- The senior team selected their top six focal questions.
- The core team did a bit more wordsmithing and boom! Six tight questions with buy-in from senior staff.

This process took two weeks, and discussions occurred during three to four meetings. We ensured that the executive sponsor and his team were on board because their voices were in each of the six focal questions.

Now you may be wondering: *"Is it okay to investigate six focal questions at the same time? I thought the whole point was to focus on just one?"* You are right. It can be daunting for a single team to work on multiple focal questions. However, if you are a large department, it IS possible for several teams to work simultaneously on their own focal issue.

Sample Focal Questions: Good/Not Good?

Now that you've learned something about focal questions, let's try a little quiz. Look at the following three questions and give them a thumbs up or a thumbs down.

1. *What will Amazon look like in ten years?*

{buzzer sound} It's not a good question for two reasons: We want to look at multiple future WORLDS, not the future of Amazon. We want to know about plausible futures in which e-commerce (and our organization) will exist—not the future of a single company. Presumably, you have some control over the organization you are in. You want to focus on the WORLD in which your organization will exist in the future. And we want multiple answers, not a single answer. So, we use "What might…" versus "What will…"

So, given that, a much better question could be:
"What might the e-commerce value proposition be in ten years for global consumers of personal care items?"

How about this focal question?

2. *What might consumers value five years from now?*

{buzzer sound} Way too broad. Which consumers? Could you segment geographically or demographically? Or focus on a segment of the consumer experience? How might the consumer purchase the product or the service?

When you're creating your question, invoke the Goldilocks Principle: not too big, not too small. Aim for a "just right" sizing of your scope.

Here's an example of a better focal question:
What might U.S. retail consumers under 40 value in a department store experience five years from now?

We've narrowed the segment and the experience.

Last one. Let's say I am the president of a small college and I'm wondering about our future so I'm convening a strategic foresight process:

when generating a focal question, focus on the WORLD in which your organization will exist in the future.

3. *What might the future of education be in ten years?*

Hmmm. This is tricky. It's not horrible, but it could be better. Education immediately puts us in the formal learning space, which makes the question somewhat narrow. But a better way to explore the topic might be to expand beyond the walls of formal education as we know it today.

How might advanced learning take place in ten years?

This opens the question to the many forms of education that have emerged.

Here are some more examples of focal questions that follow the guidelines:

How might work take place in large (500+ employees) organizations in ten years?

How might entry-level talent be managed in ten years?

What might the future of senior recreational travel be in five years?

Note the elements of scope, category, and timeframe. And that's it! You now have some ideas for getting input on your focal topic from your ecosystem and a recipe for constructing a focal question.

Future of Supply Chain Case Study

As we go through each stage, we'll build out a case study so that you will have an example built out. We've chosen the supply chain **category**. The **scope** is multi-national companies with global supply chains. We think the **timeframe** should be seven years. Here is the focal question we're considering:

> *What might the global supply chain look like for multi-national companies in seven years?*

Summary

- A focal question provides FOCUS. It defines what's in the exploration and what's out.
- When you are practicing strategic foresight, you are imagining future external worlds in which your organization will exist. You are not imagining futures of your own organization.
- The purpose of a focal question is to reduce overwhelm and help you (and your colleagues) focus your brainpower on exploring one or a few crisp questions.
- A focal question includes three parts: scope, category, and timeframe.
- Tap your ecosystem and work with your fellow travelers to create a strong focal question.
- Use the Goldilocks Principle to size and shape the question. Don't make it so big that nothing is excluded. Don't make it so tight that exploration is restricted.
- A focal question usually includes words like "might" or "could" to free your brain from searching for a certainty or prediction.

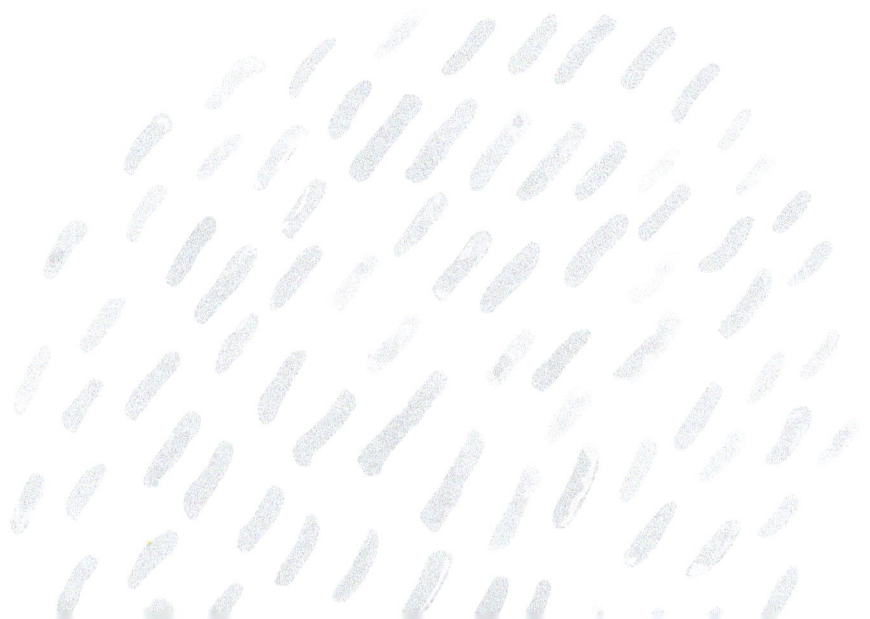

Your Turn

Here is a simple activity you can try right now.

Write a draft focal question.

Take a few minutes to identify three organizational issues that concern or intrigue you. For instance, maybe you are concerned about your future or your workforce, your industry, or an eroding customer base.

1) _____

2) _____

3) _____

Now transform them into focal questions. (Remember "might" and the Goldilocks Principle.) Your focal question might be structured like this:

How might [industry] look in [year]?

What might [industry] consumers value in [year]?

How might [category] take place in large organizations in [year]?

How might [category] be managed in [location] [industry] in [year]?

1) _____

2) _____

3) _____

Finally, refine one of these questions to make it more illuminating to explore. Consider: Are you narrowing the focus to status quo? How could you open your question to include more possibilities like "learning" rather than "education?"

For example, soft drink companies only sold soft drinks for many years. Redefining themselves as beverage companies made a fundamental difference to their futures.

From:
What might the soft drink experience be in [year]?

To:
What might the beverage experience be in [year]?

Consider your own industry. Might you broaden the definition?

What might the [industry] experience be in [year]?

_____

_____

_____

_____

_____

_____

_____

_____

Congratulations! You just created your first focal question.

S2: Scan for Clues to the Future

WHAT IS A CLUE?

If you're a fan of mystery books or enjoy solving puzzles you already know the answer. A clue is a piece of evidence (think NCIS), or data (think ENIGMA machine), or hints (foreshadowing by a writer) used to solve a mystery. And isn't the future a grand mystery?

No one can predict the future with accuracy. That's why long-term planning is so challenging. The future remains a mystery to us until we are in it. But don't despair.

All around us are clues to the future and how it might emerge. This stage is about scanning the horizon to find those clues so we can better discern how the future is unfolding.

For example, you're a psychiatrist and you're hearing about psilocybin. The state of Oregon approved the use of therapeutic mushrooms for mental health treatment. Does your practice need to get involved in any way?

The clues are always there. The trick is filtering out the noise and focusing on the clues that matter most. That is what we'll discuss in this chapter.

In strategic foresight, we consider a variety of clues.

Trends

Trends are patterns or direction over time. We can look at their speed and how fast they grow or decline.

Some trend data are well-understood. We can extrapolate from demographic and historical data. For example, by looking at global birthrates we can conclude:
*In Africa, the average age is 19 years old and rapidly getting younger. The continent is growing so quickly that by halfway through this century, it will be home to one billion children. By 2050, **two in every five** children in the world will be born here* (World Economic Forum).

Actuarial tables are also well understood. Experts can estimate life expectancy based on huge samples of data. For example:

The average life expectancy for a cisgender female born in the United States in 2025 is projected to be a median of 85.2 years. There has been a steady increase over the past thirty years in the average cisgender female life expectancy in the U.S. (Social Security Administration).

This type of data is not accurate in predicting on an individual basis, but they are helpful in anticipating, say, when there are enough schools or enough people for the upcoming labor force.

Innovation Trends

Innovations are new ideas, new business models, new ways of doing something that have been introduced or discovered. Many of the trend data you will gather are from innovations and how they are deployed.

Examples:

The FDA has approved RelieVRx, a prescription use virtual reality experience that helps patients adjust their cognitive, emotional and physical responses to chronic pain. RelieVRx is the first and only FDA-authorized at-home immersive virtual reality (VR) pain treatment indicated as an adjunctive treatment for chronic lower back pain (https://www.relievrx.com/2025).

The global manufacturing sector continues to suffer from labor shortages according to the International Labour Organisation (ILO). One of the main drivers is demographic change, which is already burdening labor markets in leading economies such as the United States, Japan, China, the Republic of Korea, and Germany. Although the impact varies from country to country, the cumulative effect on the supply chain is a concern almost everywhere.

The use of robotics significantly reduces the impact of labor shortages in manufacturing. By automating dirty, dull, dangerous or delicate tasks, human workers can focus on more interesting and higher-value tasks (Robotics, 2025).

WHAT IS A FUTURIST?

I once heard someone criticizing futurists saying, "I don't put stock in futurists—they have a terrible track record of predicting the future." Futurists are the first to tell you that they do NOT make predictions. So, what DO they do?

In the words of the wonderful Amy Webb: "They make projections in order to create a state of readiness, to determine strategic actions, to aid in decision-making, to build long-range plans, or to simply imagine alternate future states" (Webb, n.d.).

Amy Webb calls herself a quantitative futurist. She and her amazing team at the Future Today Strategy Group publish Tech Trends annually and share them online and in webinars. Don't miss them.

Jonathan Brill is described as a disruptive strategist. He's got a fascinating background and wry sense of humor which pops out in his book, Rogue Waves. In the book, Brill shares well-told insights to the changing forces in the world and a blueprint for how to future-proof your business. Disruption will come, he argues, and sudden threats can create outsize opportunities for organizations who prepare.

"Weak Signals"

These are early indicators of a trend that may become significant in the future. They are low-intensity information that heralds a trend, a threat, or an opportunity. Weak signals are the golden ticket of scenario work because they are not yet mainstream or widely recognized.

For example, the Seasteading Institute is building floating societies with significant political autonomy. Nearly half the world's surface is unclaimed by any nation-state, and many coastal nations can legislate sea-steads in their territorial waters (Seasteading Institute, 2025).

Will these floating societies become commonplace? Who knows? But a few of us are watching with interest.

WEAK SIGNALS

By definition, weak signals are difficult to sense. It's as if we're in a remote desert location and we have to move around to get a signal. But WHY are they weak? These signals are weak for at least two reasons. They are:

Hard to detect

Hard to recognize

Hard to Detect

An innovation is difficult to detect if you are not in the vicinity. We know less about other geographies, and we know less about other domains. That's why futurists and "cool hunters" spend a lot of time scanning far-flung sources for emerging indicators. This is a capability that you can develop—especially as a team practice.

Hard to Recognize

You know all those stories about experts who fail to see signals of disruption? For instance, how could the Swiss watchmakers, the world's leaders, be rivaled (first by the electronic wristwatch they developed and more recently by the Apple watch)? How could Kodak have underestimated the impact of the instant picture camera from Polaroid?

Both personal biases and organization biases get in our way. As Paul Schoemaker and George Day note, "whenever multiple pieces of evidence point in opposite directions, or when crucial information is missing, our minds naturally shape the facts to fit our preconceptions" (Day, 2009).

How to Scan for Clues Online

Prior to the early 1990s, we relied on libraries and subscriptions and a slow dissemination of breaking trends.

The good news is that, today, you can find information about lots of trends in a matter of seconds. The bad news is that it's easy to get overwhelmed by what you find. Not to worry. As you practice, you'll be able to weed through masses of data and keep track of the handful of clues that are most relevant. Over time, you will develop savvy around spotting early signals that will evolve or die.

Beyond what we can access via AI or the internet, we live in a time when many organizations publish beautifully researched reports and give them away for the price of your email. If you're willing to pay for a subscription, you will have access to more articles and reports. Be aware that these reports may or may not have an editorial bias.

Speaking of biases, this is a good time to talk again about the importance of engaging with others. You may have a bias about what you find interesting. You may love watching tech trends. But your eyes glaze over at legislative trends. You're much better off working in teams with a mix of interests so that you are not caught off guard. Those closest to an innovation or process or any other business phenomena are often the last to see early signals—because of their biases.

AI and Scenario Work

Can AI help you with strategic foresight? Absolutely! Are there any concerns? Yup.

By now you have probably used AI. It's amazing, right? And you also know there are some cautions when using them:

1. Information you receive may not be the most current. The AI models aren't trained on proprietary sources such as current research or some resources with paywalls.
2. These models are trained on material that contains human biases and reflect those biases.
3. Relying solely on input from your favorite LLM can weaken your writing and analytical skills.

> "Coupling technology with human intelligence and judgment, organizations will be able to better foresee risks and turn them into opportunities."
>
> TONNY DEKKER, EY GLOBAL CONSULTING ENTERPRISE RISK LEADER

Creativity and imagination are fundamentally human traits that AI lacks. As a result, it may struggle to generate scenarios for highly unconventional or unprecedented situations that require creative thinking.

Most importantly, when you shop out the work to AI, you miss one of the biggest benefits of strategic foresight: the fundamental shift that occurs in your mental models as you collaborate with others to generate and analyze the implications of strategic foresight work. If you're relying on AI to do all the work for you, you're not re-mapping your thinking. You're reading someone else's work, and that's unlikely to have much impact.

That said, we DO use our favorite LLMs to do some initial searching. Asking for a 'Top 10" list of something can send us down a different path where we discover a new (to us) trend or area of exploration.

Here's a bit of advice from one of our favorite LLMs, Claude: *The most sophisticated trend search methodologies combine multiple AI tools in sequence. Start with broad pattern recognition in large language models, then deploy specialized tools for sentiment analysis and statistical validation of emerging trends. This multi-layered approach helps distinguish between fleeting phenomena and substantive shifts with long-term implications. When conducting AI-assisted trend searches, always include specific requests for conflicting evidence and counter-trends to avoid confirmation bias and ensure a balanced perspective on future possibilities.*

> "Fortune favors the prepared mind."
>
> LOUIS PASTEUR, FRENCH SCIENTIST AND MICROBIOLOGIST

Organizing Your Searches: PESTLE Framework

A strategic framework can help structure your horizon scanning. One common tool is PESTLE, which organizes and analyzes macro-environmental factors to ensure a comprehensive scan. Various versions of this analysis exist—choose the one that best fits your context. The key is to guide your data gathering to cover all relevant areas.

P	POLITICAL	This has to do with what governments are doing and how that might impact your focal question. It can include tax policy, trade restrictions, tariffs, and environmental restrictions imposed by governments. It can also include political stability or instability.
E	ECONOMIC	This has to do with local and global economic factors impacting your focal question. It can include exchange rates, cost of capital, economic growth or decline, inflation rates, interest rates, cost of living, labor costs, and consumer spending habits.
S	SOCIAL	This has to do with culture, the choices people make, and the relevance to your focal question. It can include lifestyle factors, values, career attitudes, health consciousness, consumer trends, tastes and habits, social movements, and demographic trends, such as population growth rates and age distribution.
T	TECHNOLOGY	This has to do with technological impacts on your focal question. It can include R&D spend, automation, technology incentives, and the rate of technological change, as well as social networking, robotics, artificial intelligence, and security.
L	LEGAL	This has to do with changing laws and how they might impact your focal question. It can include labor law, environmental law, discrimination law, consumer law, antitrust law, employment law, and health and safety law.
E	ENVIRONMENT	This has to do with the changing physical environment and how it impacts your focal question. It can include weather, climate change, corporate social responsibility, ethical sourcing, transportation, procurement, supply chain management, and future pandemics.

INTERNET LORE AND DATA YOU CAN TRUST

We often used to cite this fascinating quote by Jerome Bruner, a respected cognitive psychologist, in our materials: "A fact wrapped in a story is 22 times more memorable." Many sources, including reputable sites, are using this powerful statistic. While writing this book, we tried in vain to find the original source of the research to cite. Another writer was dogged in her efforts (Patience-Davies, 2021). Alas, the statement appears to be apocryphal.

Where can you find trustworthy data? That's an important question. Many search engines use algorithms that show you more content based on your previous interests, which can lead you to unreliable sources and reinforce existing biases.

There are similar frameworks to PESTLE, including:

STEEP: A STEEP analysis includes social, technology, economic, environmental, and political categories.

STEEPLE: A STEEPLE analysis includes everything in PESTLE with the addition of ethics as its own category. Some examples of the ethics category include social and cultural values, environmental ethics, and medical ethics.

More recently, organizations have created their own strategic framework versions. The Future Today Strategy Group works with a set of eleven "Sources of Macro-Disruption" that includes media and telecommunications (Future Today Strategy Group, 2022).

Methods to Organize
It doesn't matter how you organize your data. It *does* matter that you organize it. In all cases, it's helpful to include the source for each entry in case you want to go back for a deeper look.

Low-Tech
A simple approach is to create a spreadsheet with PESTLE framework headers and share it digitally. However, interactive tools now offer more engaging alternatives.

Online Platforms
Miro, Zoom, Teams, and Mural all have whiteboards and expanding canvases to mimic the live experience of slapping sticky notes on a wall. The advantage to using one of these platforms is the ability to slot factoids into the scenario quadrants later (see *S6: Write the Stories*).

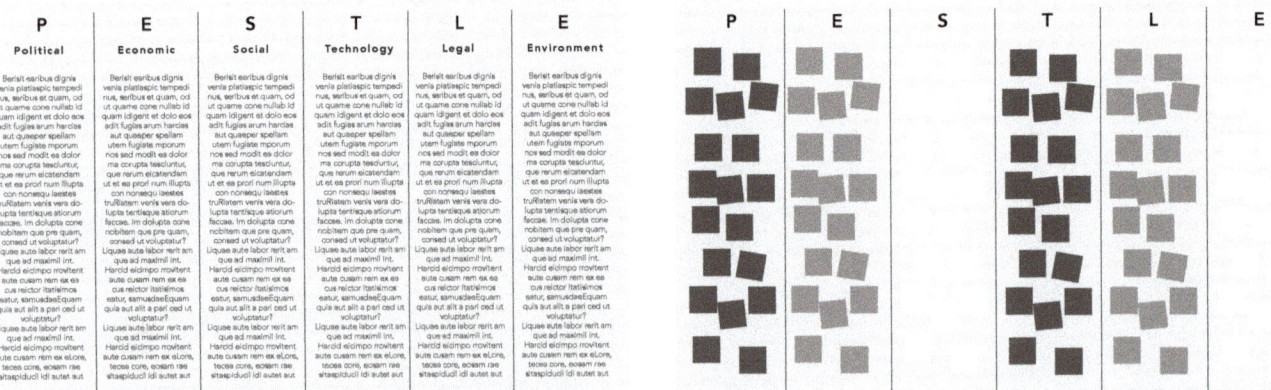

Many Hands Make Light Work

Right now, you might be thinking, *"What the heck?! How is one person supposed to do this work?"* Good question. And the simple answer is that a single person shouldn't do this work. Scanning for clues and capturing trend examples is best done by that fabulous group of fellow travelers we discussed earlier in this book. *So, should our finance expert search online for finance clues?*

Another good question! Certainly, the expert on your team will understand the implications of obscure and arcane data. On the other hand, they might have a relevance bias. That is, they may ignore something that indicates a weak signal. If you are doing concentrated research in support of a current foresight project, we recommend sticking with people's subject matter expertise. If you and your function are trying to create an ongoing discipline of trend watching (more on that later), we encourage you to shake it up. Have non-experts track a specific topic and then rotate responsibilities.

Responsible Sources

Ah, the internet. So many voices. So little oversight. How do you know who to trust? There are many responsible sources you can rely on for your trend scanning. Here are a few recommendations to get you started.

Public Agencies and Not-for-Profit Organizations
- World Economic Forum
- World Health Organization
- United Nations

Business Databases
You may be thinking that databases aren't relevant now that we have AI. However, many databases are proprietary and LLMs may not be trained on their content. Depending on your research focus, you may still find focused databases helpful. Here is a partial list of databases that can provide historical and current data on businesses and industries. Many also offer research from a wide array of businesses.

If you work for a larger corporation, you may have access to information resources and perhaps someone to help. If not, you can leverage the public library, which will likely carry many of the databases below. If you have a library card, you are (in most cases) considered a patron, and many libraries will allow you to access research tools remotely. If not, get old-school and visit your local public or university library.

- ABI/INFORM
- Bloomberg Professional
- Business Insights: Global
- Business Source Premier
- D&B Hoovers
- Gartner
- Mintel Academic
- Passport GMID
- World Bank eLibrary

Firms and Publications

Many firms are now sharing reports based on their own or cooperative research and data gathering. They also have segmented email topics worth subscribing to in addition to these online resources. There are a LOT of sources, here are a few organizations to explore:

- Our World in Data
- Statista
- McKinsey & Company
- PwC
- IEA Global Energy Review
- Future Today Strategy Group
- Deloitte
- Science News
- Axa
- Oliver Wyman
- The Guardian
- Harvard Business Review
- Millenium Project

Interesting Voices and Podcasts

There are many experts out there, whether philosophers, futurists, or writers who have likely spent zillions of hours researching your topic of interest. We've found that although podcasters come and go, many are fantastic and are worth seeking out.

Voices & Newsletters
- David Mattin:
  New World Same Humans
- Peter Diamandis:
  Future Loop
- Charles Eisenstein
- Gerd Leonhar
- Henry Coutinho-Mason

Podcasts
- What Next: TBD | Tech,
  power, and the future
- The Future of Supply Chain
- Columbia Energy Exchange
- The Economist
- Possible
- The Futures Podcast

Strategic Foresight Resources & Institutes
As demand for strategic foresight grows so do the number of organizations that can educate.

- Copenhagen Institute for the Future
- Futures Platform
- Institute for the Future
- The University of Houston (and others around the world)

How Do You Know When You Have Enough Data?

This is a chance to pursue your curiosity. Don't worry about finding the "right trends." In strategic foresight, there's no "right" answer—so there's no "wrong" answer either. You'll never have full data. You'll never know if you got the best data. Just gather enough data to allow patterns to emerge.

When we work with teams on strategic foresight projects, we suggest a minimum of twenty strong "factoids" for each PESTLE category. That's because we're usually on a timeline, and twenty is a good start.

Not all clues are created equal. First, gather basic information, meaning things that people in each area of expertise likely know but people outside the area of expertise do not.

FACT VS FACTOID

A fact is a statement that is objectively true and can be verified with evidence.

Example: Water boils at 100°C at sea level.

A factoid has several definitions. We use the word here to describe a small or seemingly-trivial fact.

Example: Today's iPhone has more computing power than NASA used to get to the moon.

Basic Factoids
- The most used password in the world is still '123456'.
- The average worker switches tasks every 3 minutes.
- People are more likely to accept calendar invites if they include emojis.
- *33% of Gen Z say they are willing to pay 5–10% more for sustainable products* (The Harris Poll, 2025).

Then, consider what trends are beginning to get noticed. What emerging innovations could possibly disrupt things as we know them?

"Emerging" Factoids
- Many companies are moving from just-in-time inventory to just-in-case inventory.
- The average employee now attends more than 60 meetings per month.
- It is becoming increasingly common to get full-ride scholarships for e-sports. Some schools now offer scholarships not only for players but also for coaches, analysts, and event staff.
- *Digital twin technology, a digital representation of a physical asset or environment, has also emerged as a key driver of supply chain growth. According to McKinsey, the global market for digital twins will grow about 30 to 40 percent annually in the next few years, reaching $125 billion to $150 billion by 2032* (Tovee, 2025).
- *Already a major economic force, e-sports is set to reach $7.03 billion in revenue by 2029, with e-sports betting the largest revenue contributor* (Alad, 2025).
- *Microplastics and nano plastics (NPs) are being detected in virtually all ecosystems. MagRobots have shown great potential as efficient adsorbents for NPs in aquatic environments* (Yanpeng, et al. 2025).

Finally, you don't need five sources for a single trend. Strive for breadth and variety. These "color spots" will be helpful in Stage 6 when you write your Scenario Narratives.

Scanning for Clues: Scenario Project-Based and Ongoing Scanning Practice

When a team or an organization embarks on a strategic foresight project, it may be their first time doing a trend-scanning exercise. A one-time effort is okay but it is even MORE valuable to maintain an ongoing trend scanning practice. This is beneficial for strategic foresight work, obviously, and is even more vital if you want to enable strategic foresight thinking. Regardless of your role, your industry, or your interests, you will be better prepared to contribute strong strategic foresight work if you, and perhaps others in your organization, make it a regular habit, or even part of the job, to stay informed of trends inside and outside your arena. We'll come back to this in Stage 10: Integrate and Monitor.

When you and your team have completed your trend scanning exercise, you're ready to move on to Stage 3: Identify the Driving Forces.

Summary

- We can't predict the future, but clues about how the future might unfold are all around us.
- Trends are patterns or direction over time. We can look at their speed and whether they increase or decline.
- Weak signals are early indicators of a potentially emerging trend that may become significant in the future. They are difficult to spot and hard to recognize.
- Using a framework like PESTLE to eliminate topic bias ensures your data will cover a broad set of headlines.
- Gathering trend data for strategic foresight work is best done in teams.
- Individuals and teams can expand their knowledge by creating a trend-scanning practice.
- Trends can be organized in spreadsheets or by using data management platforms. Cite sources of data to enable further review by others.

Your Turn

Assess Your Current Network

Do you have any weak ties (see *Expanding Your Network on* page 49) in your network? Can you develop a weak tie through a colleague, friend, association, or social media network? An easy way is to start with a neighbor or someone in the family.

When you are expanding your network (and there are SO many good reasons to do so), we recommend having a few questions ready in advance. Once you've established rapport with someone, consider what you'd like to learn from them. Here are some examples:

What's been the biggest challenge for your industry over the last year?

_____

_____

_____

_____

_____

What helped you address the challenge?

_____

_____

_____

_____

_____

What do you think the biggest opportunity is for you over the next five years?

_____

_____

_____

_____

_____

_____

What do you see as the biggest threat over the next five years?

_____

_____

_____

_____

_____

_____

What aspect of the future are you most excited about?

_____

_____

_____

_____

_____

_____

_____

_____

Are there sources you read or listen to that you'd recommend?

_____

_____

_____

_____

_____

_____

_____

_____

Challenge yourself to talk to one weak tie each month to expand your thinking. Over time, strive to span generations, industries, functions, and geographies. People love answering interesting questions. Leaders love talking to other leaders.

S3: Identify the Driving Forces

In the previous stage, you gathered and organized trend data. In Stage 3, you will do converging exercises to transform your data into a series of statements. This stage is about harvesting the work you did during your trend scanning. From those nuggets and factoids, you will identify themes. You are going up one level of detail, from the specific to the headline. Those themes, patterns, and headlines will become a set of driving forces.

What Are Driving Forces?

A driving force is an important factor that will affect the nature of the future environment within which your organization will operate.

Imagine that a key stakeholder has asked for a brief update. Obviously, you wouldn't want to share your entire PESTLE or STEEPLE database. You need to notch up one level. But not too big. As in Stage 1 when you generated your focal question, you can apply the Goldilocks Principle here, too.

For instance, you notice that there are several factoids about robots in different fields:

- *Workplace accidents cost U.S. employers more than $58 billion in lost wages and medical costs annually. Dangerous jobs are being replaced by AI-powered robots, and oil rigs are unmanned, except when humans visit for maintenance a few times a year.*
- *In low-wage categories that were often difficult to staff, robots have assumed cleaning jobs, room service delivery jobs, and monotonous jobs.*

- *Auto manufacturing is using cobots such as exoskeletons that enable individuals on the assembly line to "lift" large automobile parts.*

TOO BIG	JUST RIGHT	TOO SMALL
↓	↓	↓
MEGATREND: Agentic AI will enable organizations to automate a large number of processes and jobs	DRIVING FORCE: Robots are cleaning and performing service jobs and reducing workplace accidents in heavy industry	FACTOID: Infinite Kitchen reinvented fast food with a fully automated assembly line approach to fresh salad bowls

GLOBAL   LOCAL

The megatrend is too big and the factoid is too small. But you can create a statement from several factoids that is "just right."

How to Create Driving Forces

1. Begin by scanning, reading, and rereading your data. LLMs can be useful if your data set is large.
2. What factoids can be grouped together? What themes do you see?
3. Summarize the themes or headlines in clear, simple statements.
4. Calibrate the specificity/generality. Not too small and not too big. Just right.

For example, here are some of the possible driving forces from our Supply Chain Case Study:

- Geopolitical realignment and new blocs as nations shift from a multilateral to a multipolar world order
- Trade protectionism (tariffs, export controls, bans, and sanctions)
- Protectionist industrial policy measures, tariffs, and subsidies introduced worldwide.
- De-risking supply chains and adopting "China plus one" strategies to mitigate geopolitical and economic dangers
- Countries in Asia, Latin America, and the Middle East are emerging as manufacturing alternatives due to developed infrastructure, incentives, and strategic locations
- Limited upstream visibility—most companies are unaware of their suppliers' suppliers
- Climate change and extreme weather events causing economic losses
- Water scarcity affecting agriculture and raw materials
- Vulnerable maritime chokepoints affecting 2/3 of global maritime trade volume
- Growing cybersecurity threats & attacks
- Increased efficiency and cost savings driven by AI and ML
- Changing demographics impacting consumer demand models
- Displacements driven by AI and ML
- Megacities doubling in next ten years, changing packaging and convenience models
- Container scarcity and rising freight rates
- Bans on forced labor (e.g., Uyghur Forced Labor Prevention Act)
- Port congestion and shipping backlogs
- Circular supply chain and packaging redesign pressures
- Political instability in sourcing regions
- Final mile delivery continues to be a dominant total supply chain cost

- Retailer pressure for OTIF (on-time, in-full) performance
- Moving from a just-in-time to a just-in-case inventory approach
- IoT sensors for real-time inventory and condition tracking
- Digital twins for network simulation and risk modeling
- Shifting global trade routes (e.g., Arctic corridor)
- Increased regulation and product compliance rules
- Carbon taxes and green import fees
- Labor protests, strikes, and unionization movements
- Rising environmental, social, and governance expectations from investors and consumers
- Global inflation and rising input costs
- Climate risk disclosure regulations
- Aging workforce and skills gaps
- Volatility in consumer behavior and shifting loyalty
- Antitrust scrutiny of logistics mergers
- Currency fluctuations affecting global costs
- Robotics and automation in warehouses and plants
- Persistent labor shortages across logistics

"For all its uncertainty, we cannot flee the future."

BARBARA JORDAN,
AMERICAN LAWYER,
EDUCATOR, AND
POLITICIAN

Select Driving Forces

Convene as a team to review all the data and refine your thinking. At this point, you want to review all the driving forces the team has identified. Then, you will converge on a strong set of ten to fifteen. Your goal is to identify the most important drivers that could affect your focal question.

Here's one way to converge:
1. Individually (in advance) generate your list of driving forces.
2. Put each of your statements on a sticky note.
3. Everyone posts all their sticky notes. (This can be done on a physical wall or using a whiteboard platform.)
4. Do some affinity grouping (group like items with like items) and eliminate duplicates.
5. Restate the driving forces in a clear way. This is done more easily in pairs.
6. Give each team member a finite number of votes. Check or dot your own votes.
7. Reduce your group data to about ten to fifteen strong statements.

Here's another way to converge:
1. In pairs or trios, have a solid discussion about your individual lists of driving forces.
2. Collaborate, combine, and restate to a strong set of ten to fifteen driving forces.
3. Reconvene and have each subset share their first driving force.
4. Open the conversation to the group.
5. Repeat until all the initial forces have been shared and posted.
6. Vote to arrive at around ten to fifteen statements.

Congratulations!
You've generated a strong list of driving forces!

For our Supply Chain Case Study, we have combined some forces, added one or two, and winnowed the list:

1. Regulatory Complexity & Compliance Burden
2. Cybersecurity & System Vulnerability
3. Labor Scarcity & Workforce Evolution
4. Geopolitical Instability & Trade Fragmentation
5. Climate Change & Environmental Disruption
6. Digitalization & Advanced Analytics
7. Consumer Expectation Volatility
8. Sustainability & ESG Compliance
9. Logistics Infrastructure Constraints
10. Resilience vs. Efficiency Tensions
11. Cost Pressures & Inflation Volatility
12. Supply Chain Visibility & Risk Transparency
13. Technological Automation & Robotics Integration

Summary

- A driving force is an important factor that will affect the nature of the future environment within which your organization will operate and your focal question.
- Think of driving forces as themes or patterns contained in the work you did in Stage 2.
- Driving forces are not as big as a megatrend. Nor are they as specific as a "factoid." Apply the Goldilocks Principle to get it "just right."
- Add driving forces that are active in your organization's ecosystem.

This stage explores a few ways to create your driving forces. When you have a strong list of around ten to fifteen driving forces, you're ready to move on to Stage 4: Select Critical Uncertainties.

Your Turn

Scan, read, and re-read the data you compiled from Stage 2: Scan for Clues to the Future. Identify the themes and headlines, then summarize them in the spaces below.

1) _____

2) _____

3) _____

4) _____

5) _____

6) _____

7) _____

8) _____

9) _____

10) _____

11) _____

12) _____

13) _____

14) _____

15) _____

16) _____

17) _____

18) _____

19) _____

20) _____

21) _____

22) _____

23) _____

24) _____

25) _____

Now, converge the list above into a strong set of ten to fifteen statements.

1) _____

2) _____

3) _____

4) _____

5) _____

6) _____

7) _____

8) _____

9) _____

10) _____

11) _____

12) _____

13) _____

14) _____

15) _____

Congratulations! You've generated a robust list of driving forces.

S4: Select Critical Uncertainties

In Stage 3, you analyzed your trend data to identify themes. We call those themes "driving forces". In Stage 4, you will work with your ten to fifteen driving forces and transform them into critical uncertainties.

What Is a Critical Uncertainty?

A critical uncertainty is a factor that is highly important to your organization and whose outcome is uncertain and will significantly affect your strategic focal question.

Critical means it could have a major impact (positive or negative) on your group/organization.

Uncertain means it is not possible for you to predict with any confidence.

We create scenarios (beginning in Stage 5) because they can address the combined impact of multiple uncertainties. In this stage, you will get up close and personal with uncertainties that could have a significant effect on your group/organization and the focal question you developed in Stage 1.

You may be asking, *"Why is it so important to spend time identifying critical uncertainties?"* Because, as you'll see in the next stage, well-defined uncertainties become the bones of a good set of scenarios.

How to Select Your Critical Uncertainties

There are multiple ways to develop critical uncertainties. We'll share two methods, but the goal is the same: to winnow your driving forces down to four or five. Two is too few. More than five is usually too many. The next step requires multiple options, but more than five critical uncertainties make the step exponentially more challenging.

Method One: Ranking

1. First, rank your driving forces on a scale of low impact to high impact (on the focal question). This is a judgment call you can do with your team, perhaps with more research.

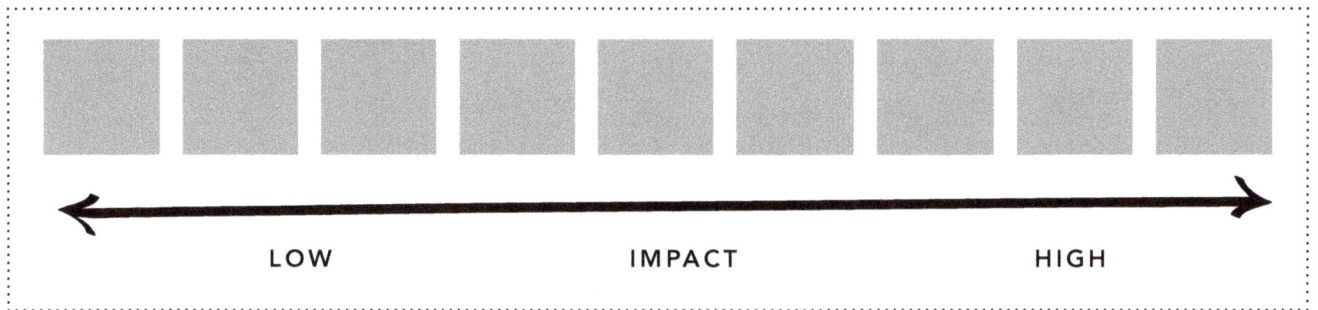

LOW　　　　　IMPACT　　　　　HIGH

2. Create a vertical axis called uncertainty (predictability), low to high. Again, this may take some additional research, and you may find you need to make a judgment call based on what you know today. Move the driving forces up according to their relative uncertainty.

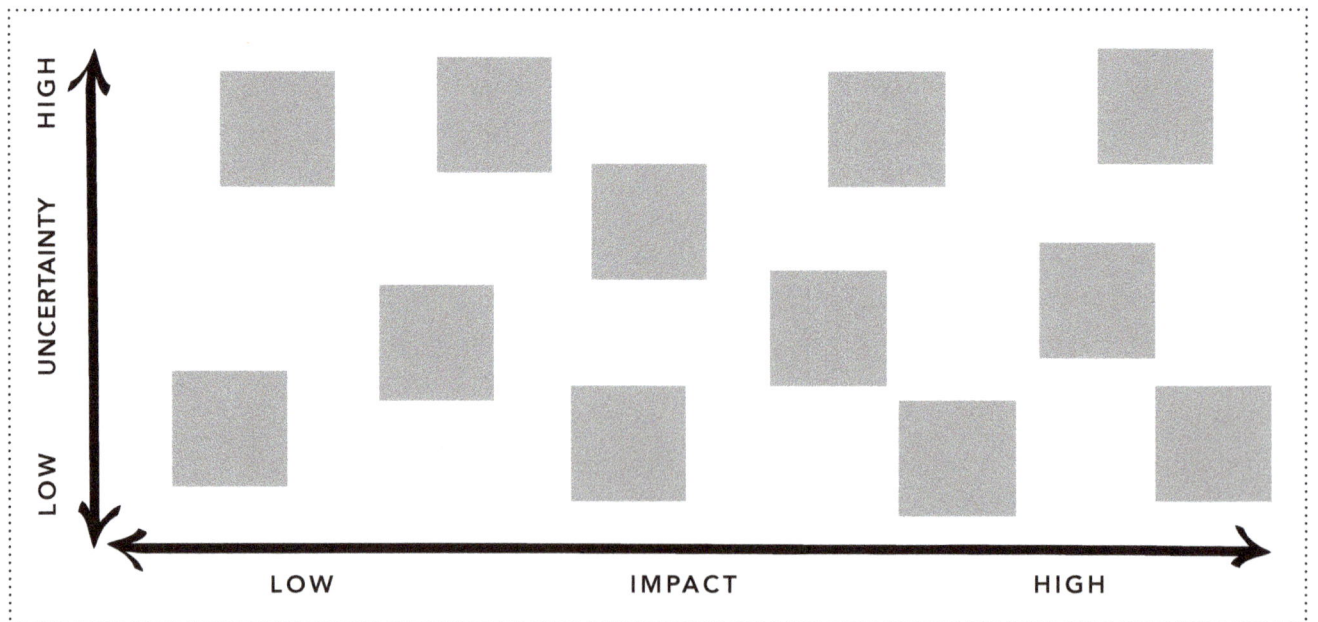

HIGH

UNCERTAINTY

LOW

LOW　　　　　IMPACT　　　　　HIGH

3. Now divide your canvas into four sections.

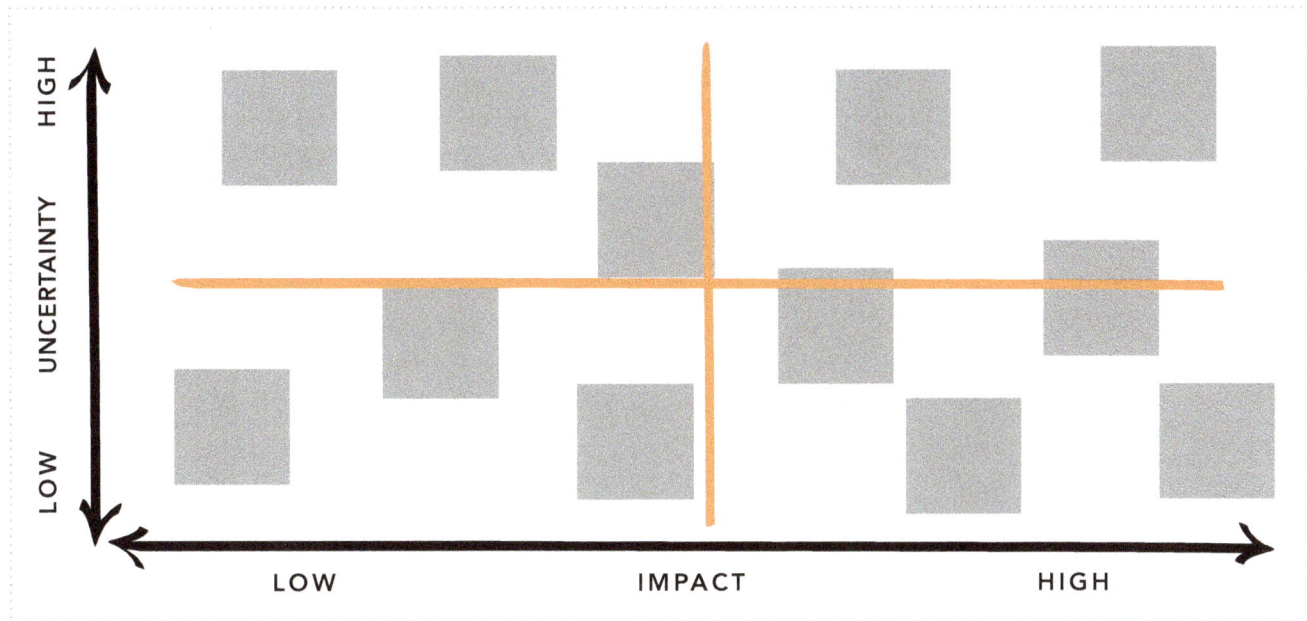

The driving forces in the high impact and high uncertainty quadrant become your critical uncertainties.

Method Two: Dot Voting and Discussion
1. Each team member gets the same number of votes. Use one color for high impact and another for high uncertainty.

2. Review the results:
   a. Any force with multiples of both colors goes to the top of the list.
   b. Any force with very few numbers or no color combinations goes to the bottom of the list.
   c. Mixed results require further discussion.

Your goal is to arrive at four to five critical uncertainties. You will first select any driving forces that are high impact/high uncertainty. If there aren't enough in that upper right quadrant, discuss the driving forces in the upper left and lower right quadrants. Again, you are considering drivers that are highly uncertain and could have a significant impact on your focal question.

Let's return to our Supply Chain case study to see elements of Stage 4 in action.

1. Develop an axis.
You've got a bucket of driving forces that are uncertain and critical. So far, they are statements. Here are a few restated driving forces from our Supply Chain Case Study as examples:
- Regulatory Complexity & Compliance Burden
- Cybersecurity & System Vulnerability
- Labor Scarcity & Workforce Evolution
- Geopolitical Instability & Trade Fragmentation
- Climate Change & Environmental Disruption
- Digitalization & Advanced Analytics
- Supply Chain Visibility & Risk Transparency
- Technological Automation & Robotics Integration

Let's look at one of these:
- Labor Scarcity & Workforce Evolution

As we're thinking about the future of supply chain work, one fundamental question is, *"Can we ATTRACT, TRAIN, and RETAIN the talent we need?"* So, our question is, *"Can we create a strong value proposition to ensure we have the talent we need?"*

Creating a strong value proposition is within our span of control so that may not be the uncertainty. It may have more to do with the workforce and the critical skills we're seeking. Are they available? Hmmmm. That feels like an uncertainty.

We know we are experiencing persistent labor shortages in transportation, warehousing, and logistics.

We know our workforce is aging and there are skill gaps and the average half-life of skills is under 2.5 years.

We know that labor strikes, protests, and unionization efforts are causing disruption in our workforce.

So maybe it has to do with the ensuring a prepared workforce, the right talent...with the skills we need. Let's try that.

———— SKILLED TALENT ————

2. Name the ends of the axis.

We believe that having the skilled talent we need in the future is uncertain. When you're naming the poles, you want to assign adjectives that are opposites. In our case, we'd like the talent we need to be ready and abundant. But we're worried that we may not be able to hire people with the skills we need. Scarcity and abundance describe this concern.

Abundant ———— SKILLED TALENT ———— Scarce

3. Develop four or five critical uncertainties.

Based on our trends and drivers, we are thinking of adding these uncertainties. They are large categories and critical to our focus question. You'll notice that not all of these map to specific drivers. That can happen. As you do your research, you may find that you've over-revved on one or two drivers and under-revved on others. As we reground on the focal question and the research, we came up with these five options:

Proactive ———— CLIMATE RESILIENCE ———— Reactive

Managed ———— TECHNOLOGY EVOLUTION ———— Chaotic

Secure ———— CYBERCRIME ———— Vulnerable

Volatile ———— GEOPOLITICS ———— Cooperative

Traditional ———— EMPLOYEE DEVELOPMENT ———— Cutting Edge

AXIS OPPOSITES

Here is a list of possibilities you can use or adapt.

Stable → Changing

Centralized → Decentralized

Internal → External

Short-term → Long-term

High-tech → High-touch

Scarce → Abundant

Customized → Standardized

Flexible → Structured

Clarity → Ambiguity

Independent → Collective

Integrated → Fragmented

WHAT ABOUT ALL OUR GREAT DATA?

You may have noticed that, as we move through these stages, we are converging on an increasingly smaller set of variables. At this stage, we can't address every nugget you gathered through your trend scanning. We can't manage large sets of driving forces and critical uncertainties. Don't worry, they won't be lost. After the next stage, we'll revisit all the goodness you've created so far.

4. Check for overlap.

If your uncertainties are similar in some way, rework them. Now that we look at these two, let's see if there might be some overlap.

Managed ——————— TECHNOLOGY EVOLUTION ——————— Chaotic

Traditional ——————— EMPLOYEE DEVELOPMENT ——————— Cutting Edge

Based on our research, we have five distinct and critical uncertainties. However, we're dropping "Technology Adoption" and including the learning and uptake of technology under the topic of "Skilled Talent". Finally, we're adding "Technology Impacts" as a broader option.

When you've landed on a set of four to five clear, distinct critical uncertainties, you are ready to move on to Stage 5.

Supply Chain Case Study

Here is the set of uncertainties for the case study.

Proactive ——————— CLIMATE RESILIENCE ——————— Reactive

Intended ——————— TECHNOLOGY IMPACT ——————— Unintended

Secure ——————— CYBERCRIME ——————— Vulnerable

Volatile ——————— GEOPOLITICS ——————— Cooperative

Abundant ——————— SKILLED TALENT ——————— Scarce

Summary

- A critical uncertainty is a factor that is difficult to predict and could have a big impact on your industry or your organization.
- Critical uncertainties are derived from your list of driving forces.
- There are several ways to identify the most critical and uncertain forces, including ranking and discussion with dot voting.

To transform the most uncertain and critical forces into critical uncertainties, name the axis. Then, name the ends of the axis with descriptive and opposite adjectives.

Ensure each axis is clear and does not overlap with the other axis.

Creating a set of four to five strong critical uncertainties will prepare you for the next stage.

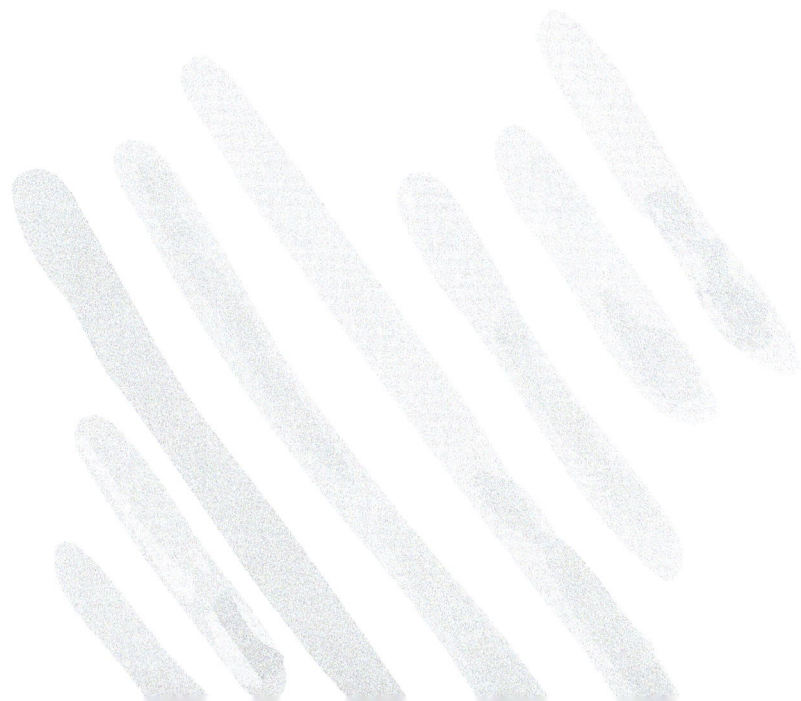

Your Turn

Look at the driving forces you generated at the end of Stage 3.

Select one that is both critical and uncertain, and give it a name.

Name the ends of the axis. Play around with the terms until you're satisfied. Try a few and see what works best for your focal question.

ADJECTIVE   CRITICAL UNCERTAINTY   OPPOSITE
                                                                    ADJECTIVE

ADJECTIVE   CRITICAL UNCERTAINTY   OPPOSITE
                                                                    ADJECTIVE

ADJECTIVE   CRITICAL UNCERTAINTY   OPPOSITE
                                                                    ADJECTIVE

ADJECTIVE   CRITICAL UNCERTAINTY   OPPOSITE
                                                                    ADJECTIVE

ADJECTIVE   CRITICAL UNCERTAINTY   OPPOSITE
                                                                    ADJECTIVE

Ta da! You just created your critical uncertainties. You are ready for Stage 5.

S5: Create Your Scenario Grid

In the previous stage, you learned how to transform driving forces into critical uncertainties. In Stage 5, you will explore how to use those four to five critical uncertainties to generate a scenario grid.

Creating a scenario grid is where the "art" of the methodology comes into play. There isn't a precise algorithm. You'll play with the uncertainties you've created and try a few options. When you land on a good combination, you'll know.

What Is a Scenario Grid?

A scenario grid is the scaffolding for your scenarios. Using two of the uncertainties, you will create a two-by-two matrix. *(Yes! All consultants love a good two-by-two!)*

Here is an illustrative example we've used in leadership workshops:

What might luxury cruising look like in ten years?

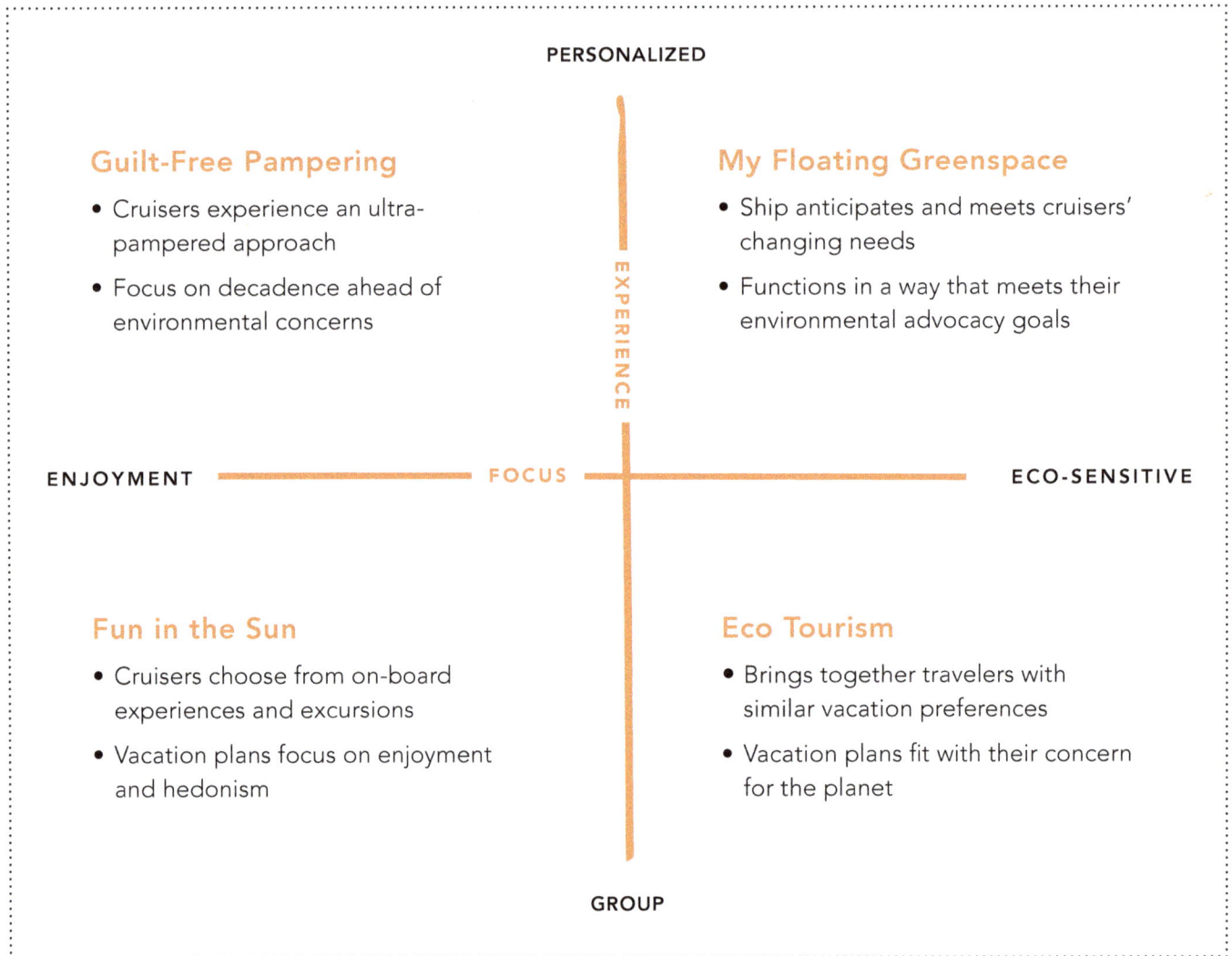

PERSONALIZED

Guilt-Free Pampering

- Cruisers experience an ultra-pampered approach
- Focus on decadence ahead of environmental concerns

My Floating Greenspace

- Ship anticipates and meets cruisers' changing needs
- Functions in a way that meets their environmental advocacy goals

ENJOYMENT ———————— FOCUS ——— ECO-SENSITIVE

EXPERIENCE

Fun in the Sun

- Cruisers choose from on-board experiences and excursions
- Vacation plans focus on enjoyment and hedonism

Eco Tourism

- Brings together travelers with similar vacation preferences
- Vacation plans fit with their concern for the planet

GROUP

This is what a scenario grid looks like, and it's where we're headed with your critical uncertainties. Let's talk about how to get there.

How to Build a (STURDY) Scenario Grid

Start with the critical uncertainties you identified in Stage 4. You can randomly select any two to combine. For the first one, we're selecting Climate Resilience and Technology Impact.

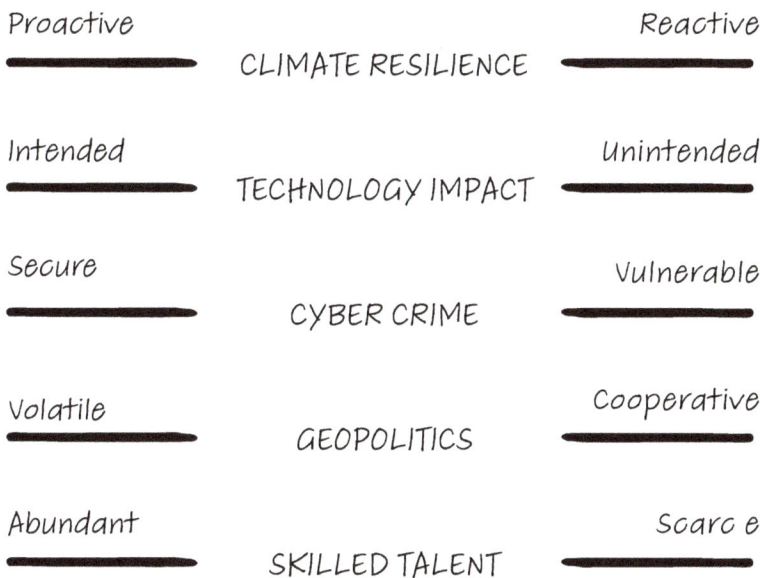

Proactive   CLIMATE RESILIENCE   Reactive

Intended   TECHNOLOGY IMPACT   Unintended

Secure   CYBER CRIME   Vulnerable

Volatile   GEOPOLITICS   Cooperative

Abundant   SKILLED TALENT   Scarce

TESTS FOR YOUR SCENARIO GRID

In this stage, you'll try multiple combinations to see which gives you the most intriguing matrix—and, in the future stages, the most useful scenarios. Here are some questions to ask at this stage:

1) Are all four quadrants PLAUSIBLE?

2) Does each quadrant have a BIG IDEA you can articulate?

3) Is the story line suggested by each quadrant DISTINCT from the others?

4) Does each quadrant imply a different kind of IMPACT on the focal question? Can you identify different types of impacts and responses on the future of work?

5) FEAR FACTOR. Can you identify one quadrant that would imply a difficult future for your organization? One scenario should have clearly negative implications for organizations like yours.

To create the matrix, we turn one of them sideways.

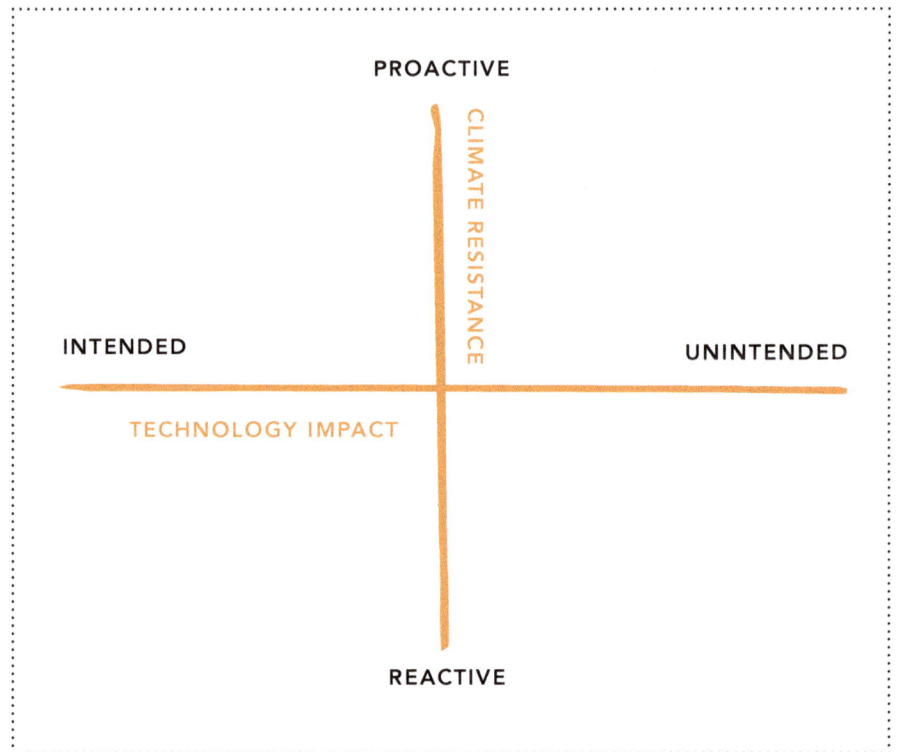

PROACTIVE

CLIMATE RESISTANCE

INTENDED   UNINTENDED

TECHNOLOGY IMPACT

REACTIVE

And voila! You've just created a scenario grid. Let's call it Option 1.

To make it easier to keep track of the quadrants, let's give them a temporary name:

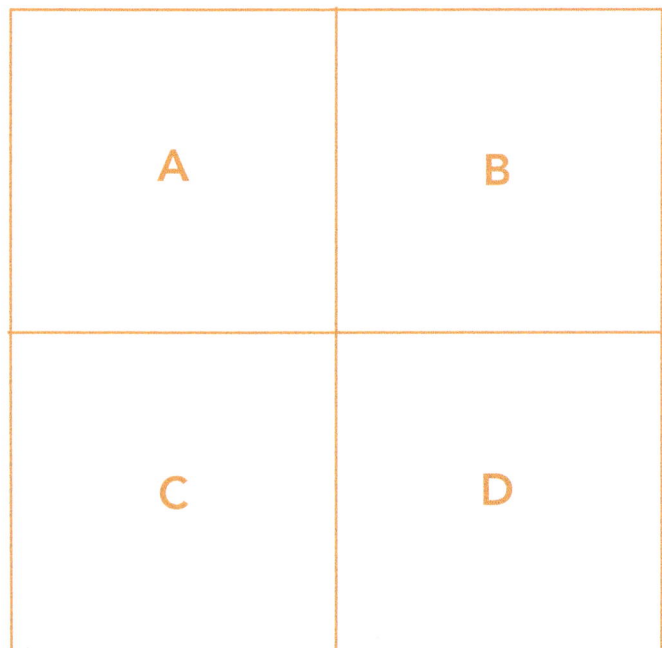

A	B
C	D

Option 1

Let's see if pairing Climate Resilience and Technology Impacts works. AI has made it possible for technology to make significant contributions to solving climate challenges. On the other hand, AI has dramatically increased the need for energy, water and hardware which isn't great. Yup, this is a chewy grid.

```
                    PROACTIVE
         A             |  CLIMATE          B
                       |  RESILIENCE
                       |
  INTENDED _____|_____ UNINTENDED
                       |
         TECHNOLOGY IMPACT
                       |
         C             |                   D
                    REACTIVE
```

Option 2

Let's pair Skilled Talent and Geopolitics.

This is also interesting. We know that depopulation is affecting many countries in the EU and Asia, especially. There is a large labor gap of skilled workers. Some are cooperating with more populous countries to import talent. On the other side, countries are actively closing borders and restricting immigration. There is definitely an interesting story to tell in each of these quadrants.

When we're exploring 5 uncertainties, we could make up to 10 distinct scenarios. However, several of these pairs overlap in small ways. Remember, we're focusing on the most uncertain and most critical to our business. Let's try Climate Resilience and Geopolitics.

```
                      SCARCE
         A              |  SKILLED         B
                        |  TALENT
                        |
  COLLABORATIVE _____|_____ COMPETITIVE
                        |
         GEOPOLITICS
                        |
         C              |                  D
                     ABUNDANT
```

Option 3

This one feels right. Climate events have a huge impact on supply chains and the geopolitical shifts make supply chain more challenging with each year. Scenario A is a world where supply chains are working together for mutual benefit. Scenario D is a world where supply chain operators have less influence on the critical uncertainties. As a group, these four quadrants provide clear and distinct worlds.

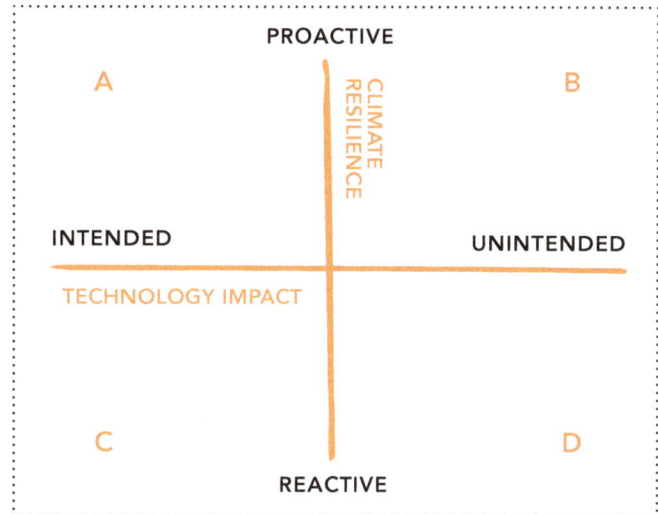

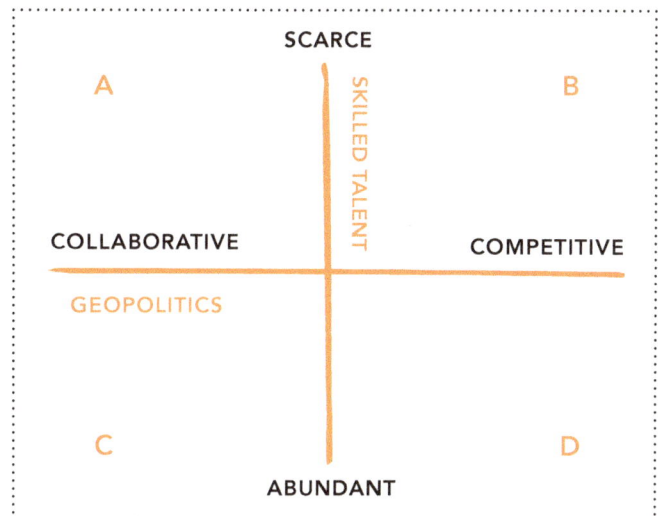

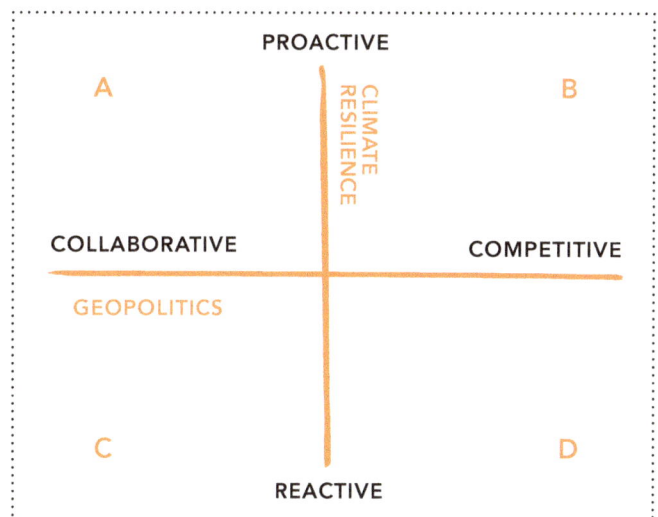

```
                    PROACTIVE
         A             |  CLIMATE          B
                       |  RESILIENCE
                       |
  COLLABORATIVE _____|_____ COMPETITIVE
                       |
         GEOPOLITICS
                       |
         C             |                   D
                    REACTIVE
```

SCENARIO GRID AS A THINKING TOOL

In 2019, Maggie had the pleasure of working with the multiple successors to the C-Suite at a global tech company. As part of their leadership development program, she introduced participants to a rapid-cycle scenario planning using a Future of Talent set of scenarios. Over the next few months, they worked in teams to explore focal questions from the CEO.

The following year, four of these same leaders mentored participants in a different leadership development program and spoke of their scenario insights and practice. The soon-to-be general counsel described scenario work as scenario thinking. He shared how he routinely created quick scenario grids to examine multiple possibilities of an issue based on their critical uncertainties.

The scenario grid, on the back of a napkin, can be a valuable thinking tool and demonstrates the versatility of thinking in multiple futures.

For instance, if you are in a planning meeting and the group is struggling to move forward because you have differing ideas about the future, sketch out a scenario grid and share it with the team. If you can agree on the two-by-two, planning may get easier.

Process Recap

Let's review the steps we took to get to a sturdy scenario grid:

1. Begin by randomly combining two critical uncertainties. A critical uncertainty is a factor that is highly important to your organization and whose outcome is uncertain and will significantly affect your strategic focal question.

2. Work from a flip chart if you're in the same room with your colleagues. Use an online whiteboard if you're working remotely.

3. Give each quadrant a letter or number.

4. Spend time with each quadrant and ask, *"What are the characteristics of this future? Explore. Finish this sentence repeatedly: "This is a world where…"*

5. Ask, *"Does this grid meet the tests of a good scenario grid?"* (See *Tests for Your Scenario Grid* on page 75.)

6. Repeat with different combinations of critical uncertainties until you agree on the combination that best yields intriguing and different futures.

This can be a lively discussion. It's not always obvious which scenario grid you'll want to use going forward. You may find yourselves renaming the critical uncertainties. You may find yourselves renaming the axes. You have permission to make the scenario grid work for you. You're in charge—not the grid.

Summary

- Build your scenario grid by combining two critical uncertainties to create four quadrants.
- Try multiple options with different combinations of uncertainties.
- A good scenario grid will create intriguing and distinct futures.
- You can test each quadrant for plausibility, sufficient difference among them, an implied big idea, varied impacts on the focal question, and the fear factor.
- Finding the right scenario grid for your focal question takes trial and error. You may rename uncertainties as you complete the exercise.

Once you finish this stage, you'll have a single scenario grid and probably some ideas about elements in each of those four futures.

Here is the scenario grid we will be using for the Future of Supply Chain Case Study.

> "If one of the quadrants doesn't scare you then your thinking hasn't been robust enough."
>
> GREG BLYTHE, FORMER SR. STRATEGIST, HP MEGATRENDS GROUP

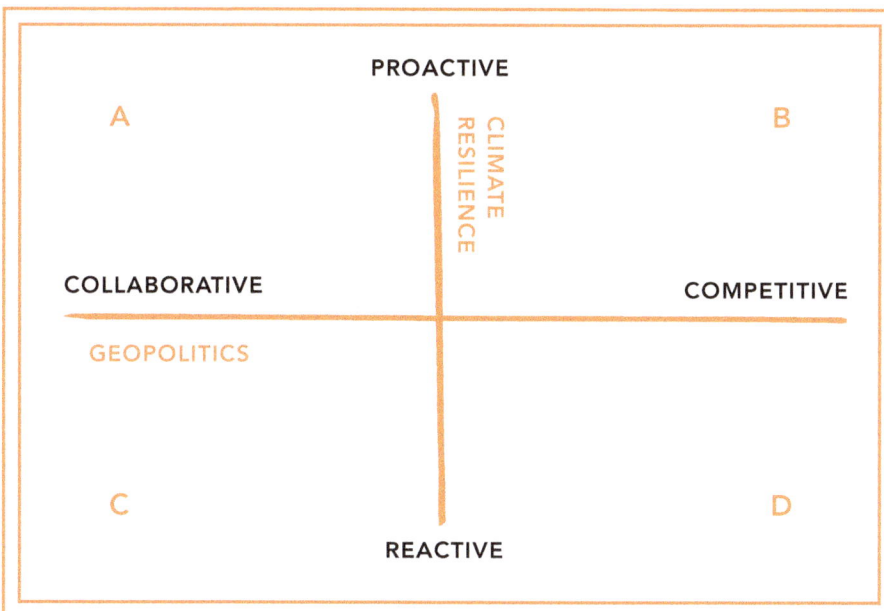

Your Turn:
Create a Back-of-the-Napkin Scenario Grid

Reflect on your organization or situation for a moment. What are a few things keeping you awake at night?

Sketch out three critical uncertainties, including the one you created at the end of Stage 4 on page 72:

| ADJECTIVE | CRITICAL UNCERTAINTY A | OPPOSITE ADJECTIVE |

| ADJECTIVE | CRITICAL UNCERTAINTY B | OPPOSITE ADJECTIVE |

| ADJECTIVE | CRITICAL UNCERTAINTY C | OPPOSITE ADJECTIVE |

Now play with them. You're not betting any money or resources on your work, so relax and experiment with the process.

Congrats! You just created a few scenario grids and used them as a thinking tool.
You're ready to move on to Stage 6: Write the Stories.

S6: Write the Stories

WHO WRITES THE SCENARIOS?

In all our leadership scenario engagements, we've observed that teams spread the work. Several team members populate the quadrants with lists. Several others write the stories. Then, all the team members work on a final version.

Some corporations, like Lowe's, hire professional writers. "We hire professional published science fiction writers, we give them all of our data, and then we send them out in all directions," Kyle Nel told Digital Trends in 2017. "And then they come back with short stories...we turn these into unexpected manifestations—usually comic books" (Kaplan, 2017).

Nel was the executive director of the Lowe's Innovation Lab and a behavioral scientist by trade. Part of his job was reading sci-fi literature and printing comic books. "I literally make comic books for our executive team, and we sit down and literally read comic books. It sounds corny, but it works," he said.

Since the Lascaux caves were painted (around 15,000 BCE), human beings have created their stories, told their stories, and moved others to action through their stories. Human beings have always been—and will always be—wired for stories.

Why? Because our brains love stories. When we're listening to facts and figures, only a small part of our brain is engaged, and we retain less. Stories light up more areas of our brain and help us retain more. When those stories are augmented with images, the brain is happy. Visual and auditory learners retain more.

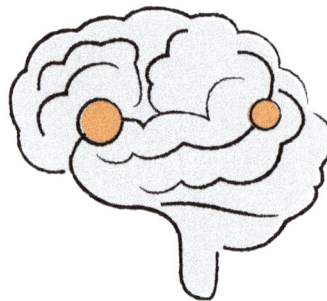

Your Brain on Facts   **Your Brain on Stories**

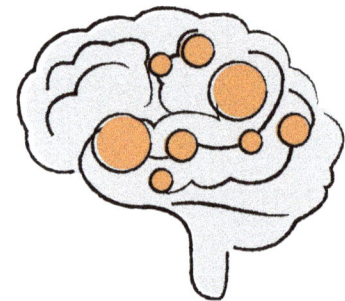

Something else happens when we read or listen to stories. Our perspectives become part of the story. We fill in details from our own memory banks and experiences.

As smart professionals, we want to believe that we follow the data and make decisions using hard facts. But when we also tap into our intuition, our decisions are even better. Stories engage our intuition. As Michael Harris, co-founder of Salesforce, shares, *"Rather than thinking of the emotional mind as irrational, think of it this way: an emotion is simply the way the unconscious communicates its decision to the conscious mind."*

Stories are one way of distinguishing strategic foresight from other forms of planning. In short-term planning, there may be a series of events, but the narrative is based on more predictable facts. They don't require much imagination to absorb. In long-term thinking, on the other hand, stories play out possibilities and make them vivid. We need to be able see and feel the future, to almost step into it, to see the implications. The best stories appeal to multiple senses.

Now, some of you may be thinking, *"But, I HATE writing! I'm just not a writer."* Not to worry. Someone on your team enjoys writing. Every time we've done strategic foresight work with leaders, there's been an English major on the team or someone who has a knack for writing. Name any group—bankers, marketeers, engineers, lawyers, salespeople—there is a writer in their midst. We guarantee it.

In the previous stage, you created your scenario grid. In Stage 6, you will use your intuition and imagination to explore the storytelling possibility inherent in each set of uncertainties.

Here, the exercise is to add color commentary to each quadrant based on the worlds you've created with your scenario grid.

A Few Words of Caution

First, it is so easy to start describing your organization in this stage. Resist! If you do that instead of describing the world, you'll immediately narrow your focus and lose the point of the entire project. You have control over your organization—well, the illusion of control, anyway. You don't need PESTLE research and driving forces to imagine four possible futures for your organization. You can already do that.

This stage is about envisioning possible future *worlds*.

You and your team will create FOUR POSSIBLE VERSIONS of the world in which your organization will operate in the future. We'll call them futures.

Scholars have studied the elements of a good story for centuries. Anyone who's watched Star wars movies will recognize familiar characters and plot elements. The hero's journey is one of the most enduring stories. Here are a few other ideas for inspiration:

Plot Elements
- Winners and losers
- Heroes and villains
- Crisis and response
- Growth and collapse
- Good news and bad news
- Discipline and freedom
- Evolutionary change
- Revolutionary change
- Cycles

Second, beware of the temptation to conclude that a specific scenario is "good" or "bad." Those qualities depend on your situation in a scenario. Instead, describe the positives and the negatives, the winners and the losers, in each quadrant.

How to Write the "Future World" Narratives

In Stage 5, you selected a scenario grid based on the criteria of plausibility, a big idea, impact on the focal question, and distinctness. You already have some inkling of a storyline or plot elements for each quadrant. This is the stage where you return to all the trend data you gathered in Stage 2—they will become a part of the stories. You can also bring in the elements that have piqued your interest and extend them ten years forward.

You did the research and learned a lot. Now, you have an invitation to create four futures by imagining, *"What might happen next?"*.

1) Start with lists.
Pull out the factoids and driving forces that fit with each future. Strive to put lots of data from all your PESTLE categories in each quadrant so your writer(s) have a lot of possibilities. As you incorporate your research, include the certainties that were filtered out as you determined your critical uncertainties. There will be some overlap given the structure of the matrix but try to put each one in the future that best fits it.

This is a wonderful time to pull out those sticky notes (live or digital) again and start moving things around.

Returning to our Supply Chain Case Study, here's an example populated with our PESTLE data and rewritten in the future.

PROACTIVE

CLIMATE RESILIANCE

- Multilateral R&D coordination accelerated deployment of emerging technologies.

- Proactive global health investments improved resilience.

- Carbon Coin piloted in Costa Rica, expanded to 34 countries by 2032.

- International Information Verification Protocol, established in 2028, aligned AI detection tools.

- Predictive analytics and harmonized building codes reduced insurance premiums in vulnerable areas by 30%.

- Digital literacy programs became standard in primary education across 72 countries. Economic incentives favoring content accuracy over virality implemented.

- Proactive global health investments improved resilience.

- Technologically advanced nations recorded per-capita climate losses from climate disasters five to seven times lower than lagging regions.

- Technological advances in water generation and weather modification became focal points of geopolitical leverage.

- Global demographic imbalances led to sustained competition for high-skill labor. Japan and South Korea pursued aggressive recruitment policies through bilateral agreements and incentive-based migration packages.

- Generative AI–enabled disinformation operations became standard components of geopolitical strategy. Competing states deployed microtargeted influence campaigns to undermine confidence. Energy systems became strategic infrastructure. Advanced nations achieved 99.7% uptime to grid modernization technologies.

COOPERATIVE —— **GEOPOLITICS** ——————— **COMPETITIVE**

- By 2032, global disaster losses reached $4.2 trillion annually. Enhanced accounting methodologies added expanded reporting to include informal economic losses and degradation of ecosystem services, which constituted 85% of total impacts.

- Heat-related mortality peaked at 890,000 in 2030, declining to 720,000 by 2032 as urban cooling infrastructure expanded.

- Lake Chad's disappearance in 2029 displaced 8.2 million people.

- Advances in medical technology became more broadly available through WHO-led manufacturing partnerships. An HIV prevention drug, expanded to 140 countries, reducing global infection rates by 70% from 2025 levels.

- In Africa, countries such as Kenya and Nigeria saw significant gains in literacy as solar-powered tablets and mobile apps delivered AI tutoring to remote areas, enhancing the reach of teachers.

- By 2028, the global economy had restructured into three competing trade blocs: American, Chinese, and European.

- Multinational corporations faced rising costs and fragmented regulatory environments, leading to reduced innovation and supply chain resilience.

- While high-income countries deployed unilateral cooling infrastructure, mortality from heat deaths rose by 40% in Sub-Saharan Africa and South Asia as international aid diminished and local systems were overwhelmed.

- Hydro politics escalated tensions in water constrained regions.

- Grid infrastructure deteriorated under climate pressure and policy misalignment. By 2032, 70% of global transmission infrastructure was beyond its design life.

REACTIVE

You'll note that the adjectives for the poles are still changing. This is typical. You can—and should—adapt your work as you move through the process.

2) Create a simple outline.
What are some highlights of each narrative? Where does conflict exist and what happens? Who are the winners and losers? You can use PESTLE as a checklist to include vignettes from each category. Because you don't have a central character, you may not have a hero's journey, but there will likely be protagonists and antagonists. Remember, you're describing the possible world five to ten years from now.

3) Write a one- to two-page rough draft of each narrative.
We suggest a very rough draft because it will change after rereading and feedback. For now, just get 'er done! You can come back and rework it later.

Begin with one future. Imagine you're already living in it.

- What is the world like in each of your scenarios?
- How did this future develop?
- Reference events from the "past" (meaning current events).
- Imagine plausible events that extend from today's headlines—climate events, regulatory action, social trends.
- Stand in the future and look back over major events—include them in the story.
- Review the lists and elaborate on them.
- Take care not to blend any weak signals out of existence. We don't know if they will become strong signals, but they are intriguing, and looking at them may help us prepare for a wider set of potential outcomes to consider.

4) Restate clues and driving forces to facts in ten years.
Now, here's the fun part: Start to restate everything as if it's ten years from now. The trends, the clues, the driving forces you gathered and identified have changed into something bigger or smaller in the future. Let's look at this emerging factoid as an example:

Mass layoffs at the National Oceanic and Atmospheric Administration (NOAA) and the National Weather Service weakened global weather predictions in 2025.

This could be rewritten in at least two ways from the future point-of-view, and both are plausible. It's your choice.

Negative consequences By 2030, the dismantling of the National Oceanic and Atmospheric Administration (NOAA) has left a patchwork of privatized weather services where accuracy depends on ability to pay. A Category 4 hurricane is tracked by competing companies with conflicting forecasts, while coastal communities can't afford premium warnings. Gaps in monitoring have created a five-year blind spot in climate data, leaving scientists and the nation unprepared for accelerating changes.

Positive consequences By 2030, privatized weather services fuel an innovation boom, with AI delivering hyper-local forecasts down to the city block. Competition drives rapid advances, linking apps to smart city systems that adjust traffic and energy grids before storms. Federal funds redirected to disaster response create strong public-private warning systems, giving communities faster, more comprehensive alerts than the old centralized model.

5) Write a snappy title for each future. (You may opt to do this before writing the narrative.)

Giving each quadrant a title is an opportunity to connect your stakeholders with a familiar theme. If you use or adapt a famous title, your audience will immediately connect it with the original story you're referencing. Your favorite LLM may also have some excellent recommendations. Going back to the The Mont Fleur scenarios, the titles given were: *Ostrich*, *Lame Duck*, *Icarus*, and *Flight of the Flamingo*s. Each of these descriptive, whimsical titles captured the specific story arc for each of the scenarios.

Inspiration for Titles

Writing scenarios will tap your imagination. Remember, the point is not to write the *best* scenario or to do it *perfectly*. Compared to what? The purpose of the scenarios is to reflect your research in a creative way that prompts discussions. And those discussions can lead to action, which is the whole point of the exercise.

Movies	Books	Games	Songs	Slogans
Requiem for a Dream	Dune	Monopoly	"Livin' La Vida Loca"	Have it Your Way
Office Space	Little Fires Everywhere	Fortnite	"Respect"	Impossible Is Nothing
Mission Impossible	Lord of the Flies	Labyrinth	"Imagine"	Just Do It
Waterworld	Ready Player One	Chess	"Good Vibrations"	Be All You Can Be
Matrix	Foundation	Minecraft	"Firework"	Tomorrow Delivered
Back to the Future	Neuromancer	Stratego	"Radio Gaga"	Think Different
Minority Report		Valorant	"Walking on Sunshine"	Tomorrow is Now
Total Recall		Overwatch		
		Tetris		
		Oblivion Remastered		

Writing Tips

- Outline the data you want to bring forward.
- Take your time writing the scenarios—you're integrating a lot of disparate information. Allow incubation time as your brain works through interesting possibilities.
- Write a very rough version first. Smooth it out later.
- Don't shy away from observations, data, and storylines that might seem unfavorable to your organization. It's important to consider plausible, even unfavorable futures so you can prepare to address them.

Qualities of a Good Set of Scenario Narratives

How do you know if your scenario narratives are good? Here are a few things to ask yourself:

1. Are the stories <u>vivid</u> descriptions of future worlds?
2. Have you included familiar elements and unfamiliar elements?
3. Are the four stories different from one another? Can you imagine a different life in each one?
4. Is there a story over time? Tell us how this future evolved; include details about possible events.
5. Are the stories logical and consistent? Do they make sense?
6. Is the story possible and plausible? Can you believe it?
7. Is the story memorable? Is it vivid and specific?
8. Does the story challenge your assumptions about how the future will unfold?
9. Does the set include scenarios with positive and negative implications for your organization?

> "Stories fulfill a profound human need to grasp the patterns of living—not merely as an intellectual exercise, but within a very personal, emotional experience."
>
> ROBERT MCKEE, SCREENWRITER

Add a "Day in the Life" to Each Future

Writing a day in the life for each scenario helps your stakeholders connect with the humanity of each story. Imagine a specific person in your future and their role. Describe their day. Describe their background.

QUESTIONS TO DEVELOP A DAY IN THE LIFE

PRIORITIES:
What is most important to them?
What do they need?
What do they most value?

CONTEXT:
Where are they?
What technology do they access?
What tools do they employ?

FEELINGS:
What do they want to experience?
How do they feel?
What do they believe?

OPPORTUNITIES:
What challenges do they face?
What would improve their experience?
What do they enjoy?

> "Data can persuade people, but it doesn't inspire them to act; to do that, you need to wrap your vision in a story that fires the imagination."
>
> HARRISON MONARTH, GURUMAKER INC. FOUNDER AND PRESIDENT

Answering these kinds of questions will help you create a realistic description of an actual human being five to ten years from now. This kind of peek into an individual's life lets your audiences enter the futures more easily.

To see a current example of a completed scenario narrative and day in the life examples for our Future of Supply Chain Case Study, please visit this site.

Summary

- Scenario narratives are stories. People have shared stories since the Cro-Magnon Era, and the human brain thrives on stories.
- The scenario grid is built on critical uncertainties. In this stage, you add certainties and detail to your narratives.
- Scenario narratives about the futures come from your trend data, driving forces, and imagination.
- Avoid "good" or "bad" scenarios. Every future will have winners and losers.
- Strive for a one- to two-page version of each scenario.
- A brief "day in the life" vignette about a specific person in the future will help stakeholders connect to the plausibility and humanity of the future.

After you complete this stage, you'll have four scenarios and a "Day in the Life" for each scenario. And you're ready to move on to Stage 7: Analyze for Risks and Opportunities.

Your Turn

Revisit the scenario grid you sketched at the end of Stage 5. Spend a moment with a couple of quadrants and imagine the world in five to ten years. Note a few characteristics about the futures.

Just for fun, give a few of them a title.

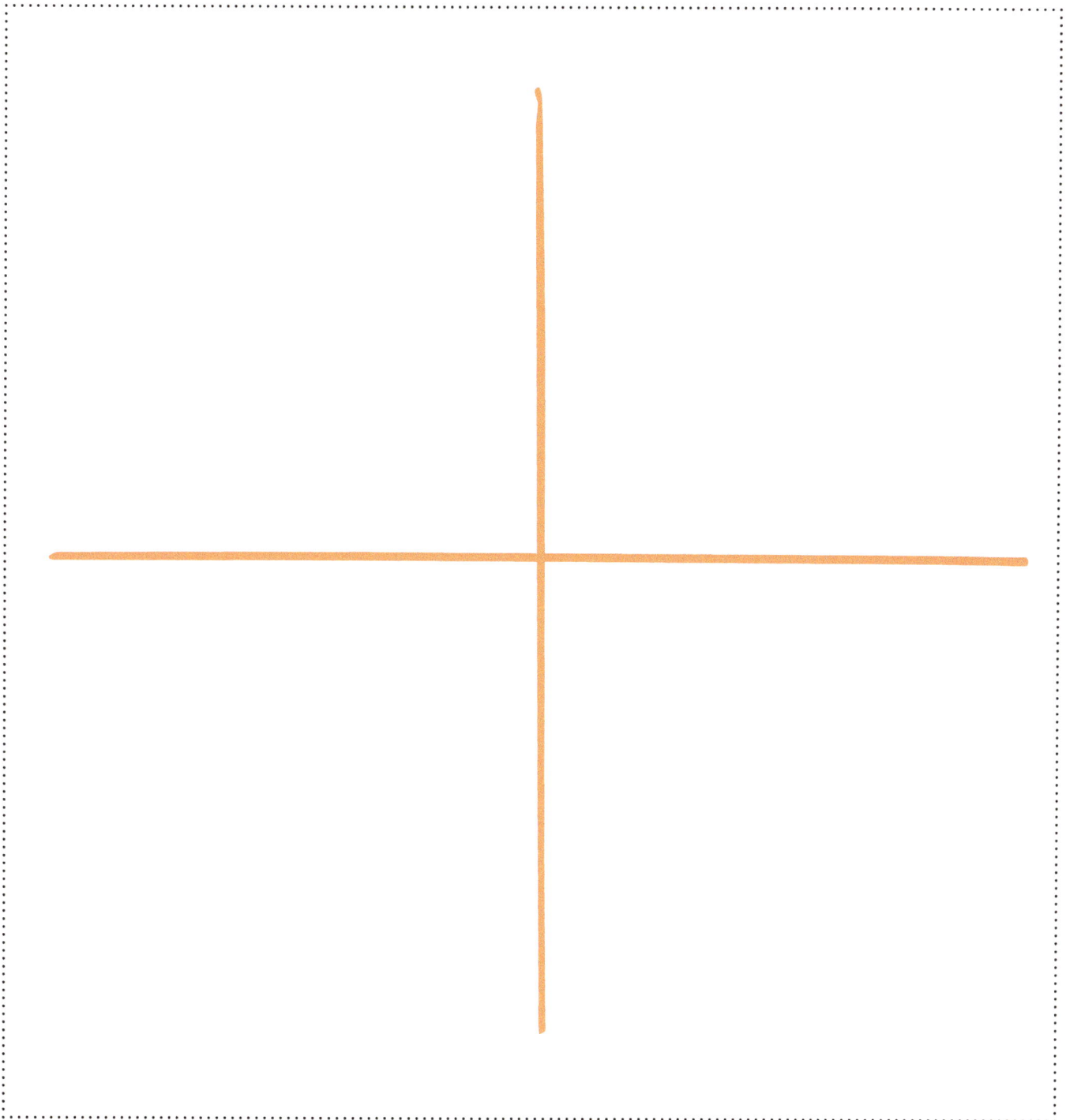

S7: Analyze for Risks and Opportunities

While it's important to create quality scenarios, they are not the end goal of strategic foresight. The goal of strategic foresight is to envision possible futures based on today's trends and then decide how your unit or organization should best respond.

In Stage 7, you will analyze each of your scenarios and explore your risks and opportunities in each future. There are two parts:

1. Assess your organization's preparedness to thrive in each future.
2. Analyze the implications for your organization in each future.

You'll begin by reading each scenario narrative. Take time to imagine you are five to ten years into the future and experiencing this world. Sink into the zeitgeist of each future.

Ask yourself: *What is it like to live and work in this world?*

Get familiar with each future.

Assess Your Preparedness

Once you can imagine each future, ask yourself: How well does your current strategy address the possibilities of each of the four scenarios?

As an example, we'll return to our Future of Supply Chain Case Study scenario narratives and assess our current level of preparedness on a scale of one (unprepared) to seven (fully prepared).

Imagine that you are a mid-size consumer goods corporation with manufacturing in Southeast Asia and corporate hubs in the United

States, Germany, and Mexico City. You have a complex supply chain operation with a mix of owned and contracted assets. Here are some of the key issues you're facing:

Scenario A: Your manufacturing infrastructure in Southeast Asia is exposed to intensifying heat waves and flooding. Tariffs and international trade laws are becoming increasingly complex.

Scenario B: Your global logistics network faces exponential cyber risks with incompatible systems across regions.

Scenario C: With wet-bulb temperatures exceeding survivability across 15% of Southeast Asia, manufacturing is taking a hit. Your energy-intensive dyeing and finishing operations face unpredictable water and power availability.

Scenario D: Competing trade blocs are reducing efficiency. Geographic instability is rising. Water access 'weaponization' means you can't rely on access for manufacturing. Furthermore, geopolitical skirmishes make sourcing raw materials difficult.

After a lot of discussion and/or averaging individual scores, you see that you are least prepared for Scenario D. Current trends paint a bleak picture. But that's good, right? Remember, if you've done your work well, one of the scenarios should reveal implications that you've not uncovered previously. Better to know this now than when you're confronting a future for which you're underprepared.

Meanwhile, you can see some opportunities for strategic partnerships in Scenario A. Further, Scenario B might lead to exploring safer or upgraded assets in new geographies.

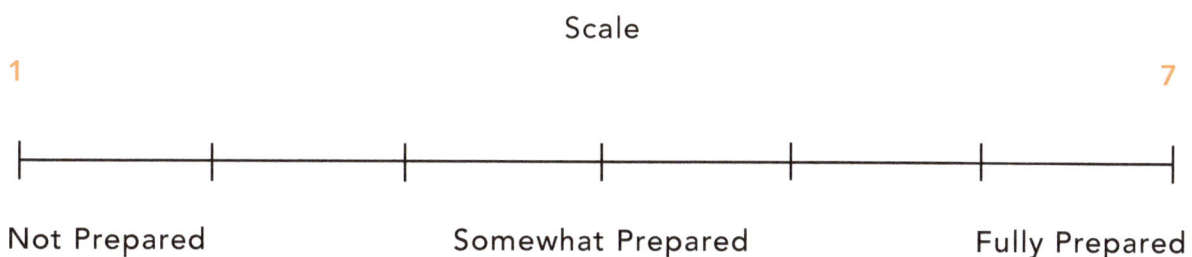

Scale

1   7

Not Prepared   Somewhat Prepared   Fully Prepared

PROACTIVE

A: Managed Transition

5

B: Techno-Sovereign Race

5

CLIMATE RESILIENCE

GEOPOLITICS

COOPERATIVE

COMPETITIVE

C: Multinational Crisis Response

4

D: Fragmented Adaptation

2

REACTIVE

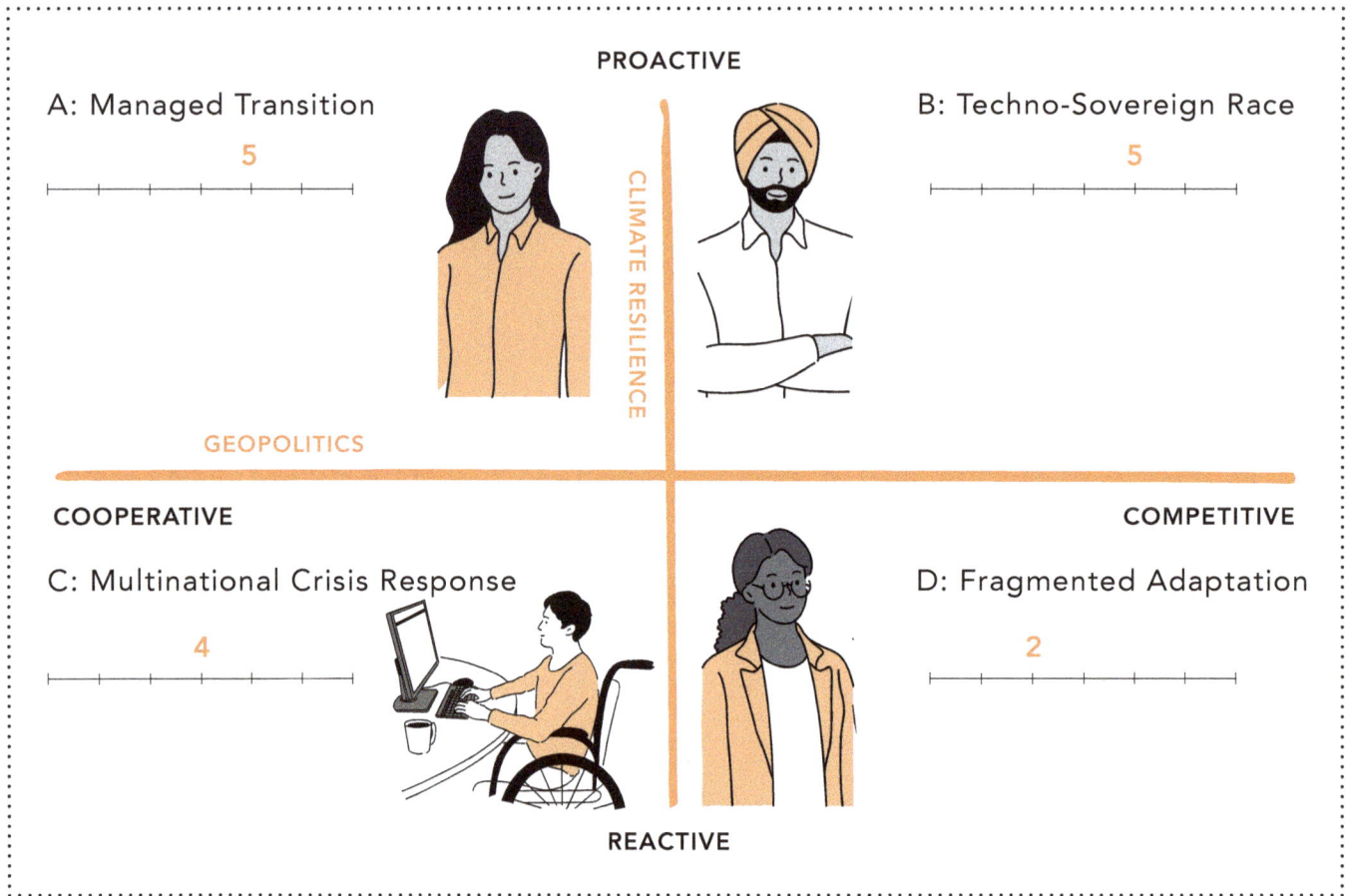

Analyze Implications

Ask: *"What are the risks to your organization in each future? Where is there opportunity for your organization in each future?"*

You can do this as a general discussion. Or you can approach this in a more structured way, as follows:

1) Use the PESTLE categories to do a complete scan.
If this future comes true, what are the political risks for us?
If this future comes true, what are the economic risks for us?
If this future comes true, what are the social risks for us?
And so on.

2) Use your ecosystem map to analyze the potential risks.
How will this impact our customers?
How might our competitors respond?
And so on.

3) Examine your organizations' functions.

What might the gaps or vulnerabilities in our supply chain be?
What might the gaps or vulnerabilities in our sales team be?
What might the gaps or vulnerabilities in our finance team be?
What might the gaps or vulnerabilities in our talent management be?
And so on.

Then ask yourself, *"What are the opportunities in each future?"*

1) Use the PESTLE categories to do a complete scan.

- If this future comes true, what are the political opportunities for us?
- If this future comes true, what are the economic opportunities for us?
- If this future comes true, what are the social opportunities for us?
- And so on.

2) Use your ecosystem map to analyze the potential advantages.

- How might this possible future positively affect key strategic partnerships?
- How might this possible future positively impact top suppliers?
- How might this possible future positively impact our labor relations?
- And so on.

3) Examine your organization's functions.

- What might the strengths and advantages in our supply chain be?
- What might the strengths and advantages in our sales team be?
- What might the strengths and advantages in our finance team be?
- What might the strengths and advantages in our talent development be?
- And so on.

Once you've spent time with each future, you'll have a list of implications for how your organization might be impacted in each of the four quadrants.

Competitive Analysis:
The Frankenstein Competitor

As part of this stage, you'll also want to look at possible competitor responses. But what happens when a super competitor emerges?

Roch Parayre, Ph.D., is a master strategist who has taught and consulted on strategic foresight around the world. Roch is a compelling storyteller and leads teams through a creative exercise about the "Frankenstein" competitor of the future. With his permission, we share the exercise with you as an option.

For your highest risk future scenario, *imagine the perfect competitor—a Frankenstein-like organization that comprises all the elements of the ideal solution.*

What customer segment(s) will they target?
What value proposition will they deliver?
What capabilities and/or assets will they possess?
What competitive advantages will they enjoy?

PROBABILITIES: GOOD IDEA? BAD IDEA?

Some strategic foresight planners assign a probability score to each quadrant. Should you predict the likelihood that a certain future is more likely to come true than another?

The classic method taught by the Global Business Network does not recommend probabilities. After looking further into the practice of assigning probabilities, we learned that there was quite a lot of energy around this topic in 1991 on an open scenario forum with many recognized scenario sages.

Most did not support assigning probabilities, while a few advocated for overtly assigning probabilities because we're doing it in our heads already.

Here's the thing: None of the scenarios you've created will happen as you've written them. The actual future will be some combination of parts from each scenario, perhaps with a wild card (like a war) thrown in. The point of the exercise is not to predict a future accurately. The value of scenario work is the exploration of many things that could happen and preparing your mind and your organization for the unexpected.

If you feel moved to assign probabilities, just take 100% and divide it among your four scenarios. Compare your results with your teammates.

It could lead to an interesting discussion.

Identify the key implications— the challenges and opportunities for you—should this competitor emerge.

This super competitor may help you generate new competitive threat implications.

Summary

- The goal of this stage is to determine how your organization, on your trajectory today, will be impacted in each of the four futures.
- There are two steps in this stage: 1) assess your preparedness to thrive in each future and 2) analyze the implications for your organization in each future.
- Calibrate your analysis to the stakes involved. Bigger investments require greater analysis.
- You can assess your preparedness for each future using a scale from one (unprepared) to seven (fully prepared).
- Generate a list of implications by asking two questions: *"What are the risks to your organization in each future— especially the one for which you feel least prepared?"* and *"What are the opportunities in each future?"*
- You can generate competitive implications by describing a "Frankenstein" competitor and assessing their possible disruption threats.

Once you've completed this stage, you'll have identified implications, including:
- Potential risks and opportunities
- Competitors that may emerge
- Early ideas for what your organization can do to manage tomorrow, today.

When you have analyzed each of your scenarios, you're ready to move on to Stage 8: Identify Strategic Options.

Here are sample implications for one scenario (Scenario D) from our Future of Supply Chain Case Study:

Extreme weather events are halting manufacturing and endangering our transport operators.

Raw materials (such as cotton) are becoming uncertain in areas of international conflicts.

Water and power are increasingly interrupted in Southeast Asian manufacturing sites.

Heat extremes are becoming dangerous for our contracted workers.

Cybercrime is a real and present danger especially across multiple technologies.

Disinformation campaigns have the potential to hurt our brand and reputation.

Your Turn

Look at the grid you drafted on page 91. Identify implications, both risks and opportunities. Refer to the guiding questions on page 94 to support your analysis

1)

_____

_____

_____

_____

2)

_____

_____

_____

_____

3)

_____

_____

_____

_____

Risks

_____

_____

_____

_____

_____

_____

Opportunities

_____

_____

_____

_____

_____

_____

_____

_____

S8: Identify Strategic Options

In Stage 7, you analyzed your scenarios for implications, both positive and negative. You now have a good sense of the risks and opportunities to your unit or organization. Next, you'll review those implications and generate options to address them.

Stage 8 is about generating ideas for **actions you can take today** that won't put your organization at risk should the emerging future take a turn. You'll come up with ideas that can better position your organization for success in an uncertain future.

What Are Strategic Options?

Strategic options are alternative actions or responses to the changing environment your unit or organization may face in the four futures.

Why are Strategic Options Important?
1. Finite resources: You can't afford to spend the time or money preparing for all four scenarios.

2. Uncertainty: You can't put complete plans in place for future conditions that don't exist yet.

You may have already thought of some ideas as you worked through the previous stages. Fantastic! In this stage, you'll get more structured about generating options.

NO-REGRETS FOR ROYAL DUTCH SHELL

At the beginning of the book, we shared how Royal Dutch Shell used scenarios to anticipate and plan for the oil embargo in 1973. Shell didn't avoid the negative impacts because of their smart scenarios; they avoided the impacts because they integrated their insights into their current plans. They acted across the organization to avoid the worst effects of the oil embargo. In fact, one of the things they implemented was a no-regrets move of cutting costs across the organization when all their competitors were still spending freely.

Generating Competitive Options

When you face uncertainty and limited resources, one approach is to look at different kinds of investments. Here are four to consider.

No Regret Moves	Little Bets	Options and Hedges	Big Bets

Types of Moves

No-Regret Moves: Actions that have no downside and can serve multiple scenarios.

These moves are no-brainer options to recommend. They will be helpful no matter what scenario emerges and typically include actions like ongoing cost management, increasing operational effectiveness, gathering competitive intelligence, building skills, investing in capacity, or creating new products and services.

Questions to ask while looking across all four scenarios:
- What requirements do all the scenarios share?
- What steps could we take that would better prepare us for all four futures?

For example, any industry, anywhere can be vulnerable to cyber-crime. Investing in advanced cybersecurity and information defense is very likely a 'No-Regret' move.

Little Bets: Experiments to discover, test, and develop ideas when there is an emerging need but no known solution or best practice.

These are initiatives to invent a solution that meets a future service, product, or capability that will be required but currently does not exist. Little bets are breaking new ground. As in design thinking, you'll operate with a "fail fast" mindset. Trials should be numerous and intentionally small so that new insights drive learning and invention without jeopardizing the organization.

Examples include prototypes, experiments, market tests, pilots, limited launches, and minimum viable products (MVPs).

Questions to ask for each scenario:
- What asset, capability, or service is required to be ready for one or multiple scenarios?
- How might a series of tests be conducted that deliver new insights quickly?
- Could we use this as an opportunity for a stretch assignment for key talent?

Imagine you're taking aim at a future and you're trying little bets. Each time, you learn something new. You learn what won't work and what will work. This will get you closer to a solution.

For instance, it might be worthwhile for you to explore additional or alternative manufacturing locations. You don't need to reshore immediately. Short trials at different locations may help you make the move, should it be necessary. You might also explore alternative sources for raw materials such as cotton. When you can make products using a more sustainably-grown plant or recycled polyester, you may save money and make your climate-conscious consumers happy.

Options and Hedges: Actions that allow an organization to develop and preserve an advantaged position and acquire time to watch how scenarios play out.

These are strategic tactics aimed at specific scenarios. They might leverage joint ventures that provide lower-cost market entry or changes to projects that might add cost but provide additional flexibility.

Examples include first right-of-refusal on purchasing an asset, technology, or an organization. Options and hedges can also include locking in leverage to a future service or capability such as disposable factories (temporary structures that can be built in months versus years and shuttered with little cost).

Questions to ask for each scenario:
- What future capabilities or assets will provide an advantage for us but don't yet exist?
- What options can we invest in that will give us access to the needed assets or capabilities?

For example, it's clear that energy access and reliability are required, but not assured in multiple future scenarios. Around the world, governments and private sectors are investing in nuclear fusion. In 2023, Microsoft signed an electricity agreement with Helion Energy, a fusion startup aiming to deliver fusion power by 2028. This didn't require believing in fusion today—but it gives Microsoft a no-regret hedge if Helion delivers.

So, you might sign an early agreement with a fusion energy company. Or you might scan the locations of the approximately 15 fusion sites expected to come online in the next twenty years if you are considering major relocations.

Big Bets: Entries that would provide an advantaged position in a market space that is currently not exploited or contested.

These are large-scale commitments that may be valuable in a particular scenario. They may be risky and involve a high degree of uncertainty with a lot of value at stake. As a result, you might not act until there is more clarity around how the future is developing. Advanced research and planning give you the critical flexibility to move quickly when appropriate.

Big bets might include creating an uncontested market space, generating and capturing new demand, or seeking out a merger or an acquisition.

Questions to ask for each scenario:
- What factors in your industry need to be raised above industry standards?
- What products or services have not been offered but should be created?
- What "Frankenstein" solution might you provide?

For instance, you and your professional peers are concerned about the coming impacts of climate change. With each year, there are more 'extreme events' that endanger your people and send costs skyrocketing. You might decide to develop a resource trading ecosystem that works for your desired future. The flexibility and rapid adaptation capabilities of such a platform would be essential for navigating the various geopolitical and climate disruptions.

+ + +

"Panic causes tunnel vision. Calm acceptance of danger allows us to more easily assess the situation and see the options."

SIMON SINEK, AMERICAN AUTHOR AND ORGANIZATIONAL CONSULTANT

By definition, no one knows how to win five to ten years from today. It hasn't happened yet, so there is no exemplar to imitate. The strategic foresight process helps you see future possibilities and identify concrete actions like the types of moves we've just covered. For all four types of competitive options, it's possible to define actions that you can initiate today.

For the Future of Supply Chain Case Study, we've identified the following moves:

No Regrets – Develop advanced cybersecurity and information defense.

Establish integrated response units spanning communications, cybersecurity, and legal teams. Invest in military-grade security structures. Train leadership teams to maintain operational continuity and stakeholder trust during an attack.

Little Bets – Experiment with alternate locations and sourcing.

Explore co-warehousing in Mexico and Eastern Europe. Launch micro-pilots (3-6 months, 1.5% scale) in alternate manufacturing sites. Establish small facilities specifically for testing new automation and robotics technologies that could enable cost-effective nearshore manufacturing. Test post-consumer and post-industrial recycled cotton sources to reduce dependence on virgin materials.

Options and Hedges – Ensure access to power.

Pursue a Corporate Power Purchase Agreements (PPA) to lock in future low-cost energy while demonstrating environmental leadership. Explore near-term facilities in the US (Washington and Virginia) and UK.

Big Bets – Collaborate with select partners to create a resource trading ecosystem.

Identify and recruit 15-20 supply chain leaders to form the founding coalition. Establish governance structure and define key resources to trade. Develop the multi-asset trading hub with scenario-adaptive features, integrating application programming interfaces (API) from existing platforms rather than building from scratch. Pilot and scale.

Summary

- The purpose of this stage is to generate options that address the implications you identified in Stage 7.
- You can't prepare for each future because you don't have infinite resources, and the future IS uncertain.
- There are four kinds of actions you can recommend or select to address implications of the futures you have identified:
    1. No Regrets: No-brainers you can do today.
    2. Small Bets: Things you need to learn.
    3. Options and Hedges: Rights you want to acquire.
    4. Big Bets: Preparations you can make.

As you finish Stage 8, you now have a complete story to share about your scenarios, implications for your organization, and recommendations for strategic options. You're ready to move on to Stage 9: Communicate the Case (for action).

Your Turn

Look at the implications you came up with in Stage 7. Consider and write down No Regret Moves, Little Bets, Options and Hedges, and Big Bet moves that could address the implications.

No Regrets Move: _____

_____

_____

Little Bets: _____

_____

_____

_____

Options and Hedges: _____

_____

_____

_____

Big Bet Moves: _____

_____

_____

S9: Communicate the Case

Have you ever taken a guided walking tour? Maggie took the Freedom Trail in Boston twice with different results, and the difference was entirely due to the guide. The first guide delivered facts in a dry, academic manner, but the second was a master storyteller who brought history to life. He captivated everyone in their group—even a family with three teenagers who were two weeks into a grueling car tour of Colonial and Civil War sites. The storyteller guide didn't just recite dates and facts. He connected artifacts to the unfolding drama of history. At each stop, he built suspense: "And what do you think happened next?" When everyone responded "What, what?" he smiled and said, "We'll discover that at our next location." We couldn't walk fast enough.

This stage, Communicate the Case (for action), will call on your storytelling talents. It's a synthesis of all the work you've done up to this point. That doesn't mean you'll be sharing a detailed description of the work you've done. Chances are extremely good that no one in your audience (whether one person or fifty) wants to hear about it. They just want to know why THEY should care.

This stage is about making them care.

And if you aren't a natural storyteller, we'll review ways to engage your audience and share a compelling story.

You've probably heard this phrase before. It's an idiom common in the United States that dates to the 1920s. It means that your hungry customer will be piqued by the sizzling steak aroma (with apologies to our vegan readers) and doesn't care about the cow or the farm on which it was raised.

Over-explaining the entire process behind their recommendations is a common mistake for many teams. You and your team know you've come up with great stuff. But having great ideas and insights isn't enough. You need to communicate those ideas effectively in order for people to know that they are great. And your decision makers don't want to hear about your process.

This chapter is about shaping your communications to fit your listener's interests.

Client Story: Crafting the Executive Presentation

When Maggie began including strategic foresight in leadership development sessions, she facilitated a rapid-cycle experience and worked with real company issues. She often had time constraints (who doesn't?), but clients managed to get through the entire scenario-building process. That is, they got through the entire process of creating four futures. It was good—but not enough. Because the point is not to create the scenarios. The point is to share the insights and inspire others to make beneficial strategic choices based on those insights. And the early work wasn't leading to that. This is why we include Communicating the Case (for action) as a critical stage of the strategic foresight process. Strategic foresight work can be a complicated story to tell and engaging your audience takes practice.

Identify Your Why

You will find that you have different goals with different audiences:
- INFORM: Share important knowledge and insights.
- INFLUENCE: Make recommendations and obtain sponsorship or budget/commitment/decision.
- INVOLVE: Engage others in planning and implementation.

Your first step is to identify what you hope will happen as a result of this conversation or presentation.

Identify the Big Why

In the Scan for Clues stage, you gathered quantitative and qualitative data. Then, you identified driving forces and critical uncertainties, which led to your scenario grid. Analyzing the four futures led to insights. *These insights are relevant for your organization's future ability to thrive.* This is the overarching reason others will care. Powerful insights will generally fall into two buckets:

1. OMG—we could be in BIG trouble!
2. Holy cow, here's an opportunity that would be amazing for us!

It's likely that your case will include a little bit of both.

Assemble the Case for Action

There are a lot of possible elements to communicating the case. Instead of looking at the documents you've created so far, we suggest stepping away from the computer, grabbing a pad of sticky notes, and finding a blank wall. Alternatively, start an online board so you and your remote colleagues can work asynchronously.

Now think about everything you've learned, discovered, and developed. What elements stand out? Put them on a note and put that note on the wall/board. Do this over and over. Add things you and your colleagues want to communicate, ideas for questions you want to ask the audience, tough questions you anticipate, key drivers in your audience—anything related to making the case and delivering it in an appealing, trustworthy, and relevant way.

Now start to move those sticky notes around. Maybe an order is emerging? Maybe you've thought of a way to engage your audience? Play with this initial brainstorm a bit but don't close yet. Give your brains time to incubate.

Come back and identify the elements. Put them in a storyline. Here is one option for doing that.

SMART IDEAS AREN'T ENOUGH

One company we've worked with welcomed a new C-suite executive in technology who was a brilliant engineer and conspicuous in the quality of her presentations. She seemed comfortable in front of a large audience, bantered with the crowd, and shared information in a clear and compelling way. Not all engineers we coach are as strong. This particular executive shared that her SAT scores were extremely lopsided, with super high math scores and lower writing scores. At that time, she stated she didn't care about the "humanities" because she wanted to be an engineer. Her efforts to improve her communications were seeded when a mentor told her, "You are very smart. But it isn't enough to have good ideas. You need to be able to communicate them." She took that feedback to heart. Now, every time she has a major presentation to deliver, she enlists expert help to ensure she communicates effectively. Coaching and presentation design helped her increase her skills to a high level over time.

Build a Storyboard

Storyboards are a kind of roadmap of your presentation. They were first used at The Walt Disney Studios to graphically map scenes and shots. You needn't do anything as elaborate as an animator or a film studio. But we recommend the process because your case for action will contain visual elements. You can use slide software, sticky notes, or an online storyboard creator.

Telling the Story

You could share your amazing data in a bunch of slides.

Or you could tell a story.

Or you could do both. In fact, you WANT stories and data. Throughout this process, you've gathered data and woven it into narratives about the future. When you add imagery, your message becomes even more powerful.

Stanford professor, Baba Shiv, notes that we often try to engage people by sharing evidence and appealing to the rational brain. He adds, "Keep in mind that the rational brain accounts for only about

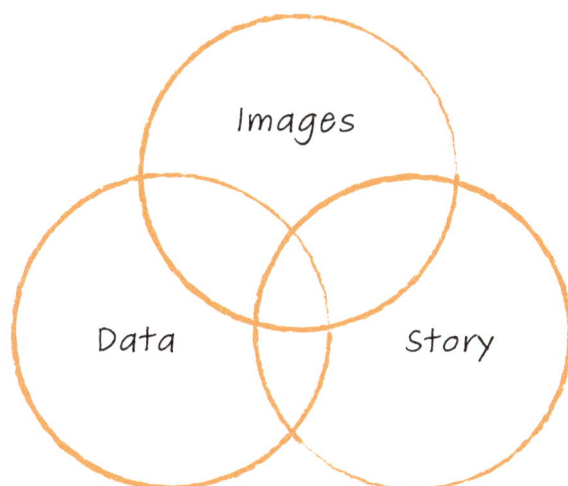

5% to 10% of human decisions by all estimates. We are not saying you can ignore the rational side, but first and foremost, you need to play into what the emotional brain is looking for" (Shiv, 2021).

That doesn't mean you have to tell a tragic story, Shakespeare style. Just draw the listener in by focusing on a real person (like your Day in the Life persona). Or describe a future partner in your ecosystem. Or a future consumer and an impact on them.

Visualizing Information

A new discipline called data storytelling has emerged. It includes the skillful blend of data, narrative, and visuals (see sidebar). The purpose is to ensure that the data has a story line and that the visuals are clear. All three must coordinate and support one another.

Here's a fun example:
Picture this extraordinary leap: global data storage is projected to explode from just 2 zettabytes in 2010 to over 600 zettabytes by 2030—a 300-fold increase in just two decades. To visualize this mind-boggling scale, imagine burning all that data onto Blu-ray discs and stacking them. You wouldn't just reach the clouds or even orbit—you'd need to build 38 separate towers of discs, each one stretching a quarter-million miles to touch the Moon itself. That's 38 gleaming bridges of human knowledge connecting Earth to our celestial neighbor, each tower representing every digital heartbeat of our hyperconnected world (Statista.com, 2025).

DATA STORYTELLING

Brent Dykes, author of Effective Data Storytelling, has been at the forefront of defining this new discipline. He writes, "If an insight isn't understood and isn't compelling, no one will act on it and no change will occur." The book is a fantastic resource filled with examples (and non-examples) of communicating a complete story.

We particularly enjoyed Brent's take on the analysis process. He suggests Indiana Jones as a metaphor for the work we are doing. We are archaeologists, exploring the data wilderness for insights. We're independent, fleet of foot and fearless. We're also professors, explaining our findings with simplicity, clarity, and cohesion. Creating your scenarios and analyzing them required you to bring your adventurous spirit and a willingness to explore. Crafting and communicating a compelling, cogent case for action requires engaging information and explanations.

Really, aren't we all a little Indiana Jones?

Humble Suggestions

Begin with an engaging opening that brings your audience into the future. This is not a status update. This is the future! It's cool! It's scary! Here are three ways you could begin to pull in your listeners/ readers:

A Day in the Life: Introduce a real person and what life is like for them in ten years. Include details about a specific thing that is easier or harder for them than it is today. One team we worked with began with the frictionless shopping experience of tomorrow for a specific person, then later compared it to the sub-optimal shopping experience of today.

Imagine a World: In this introduction, you could describe the future in a certain geography or organization. It might be a vivid description of a future with vignettes describing how your organization will struggle.

Immersion: Communicate with your audience as if you are all part of the same future in ten years. It could be a newscast, an announcer introducing the Wide World of E-sports, a fashion influencer, or a CEO presenting her "State of the Company."

Once you've brought your audience into the future, you can tell your story with more elements and evidence to support your case. These could include:

- Critical uncertainties and implications
- Frankenstein competitor threats
- New opportunities
- A high-risk scenario and a few reasons it's high for your organization
- The cost of inaction
- Two to three recommendations for strategic options (Stage 8)
- Pros and cons for each recommendation
- Signposts to track (more on this in Stage 10)

And, of course, ask questions and invite discussion with your audience.

Client Story:
What if my organization isn't into storytelling?

With one client, Maggie knew the storytelling would be an uncomfortable stretch for their culture. She offered several templates outlining how their teams could communicate the case for action (see *Assemble the Case for Action*). Recognizing that they might feel reluctant to diverge from the typical executive briefing, she mocked up three possibilities as examples. Part of each team's preparation also included presenting to fellow teams and getting constructive feedback. Thanks to their thorough preparation, each team successfully blended engaging stories with compelling data in their Case for Action. The executive panel noted that *"it's hard to be simple"* and complimented them on *"how much they conveyed in a short time."* Furthermore, they were *"nervous about the stark realities"* of the future possibilities and made plans to dive deeper during a future session.

"Those most deeply committed to, and successful in, an old system will be the last to notice a radically new idea, and will be most resistant to it. When change comes, it's the outsiders — those uncommitted to the status quo — who are poised to catch the wave."

PHILIP SLATER, AMERICAN SOCIOLOGIST AND WRITER

Format Options

How you package your case depends on many factors. Who is the audience? What does your organization culture suggest? We encourage you to take some risks in how your share your scenario work. Scenarios are an opportunity to depart from convention. Scenarios are a chance to telegraph to your listener or reader that this is not like annual business plan or budget submissions. No matter the format, you will include images, stories, and data. Here are a few options to consider:

- Executive summary
- Briefing packet
- Slides
- Live presentation
- Video
- Online static
- Online interactive

For example, if your goal is to INFORM, you're probably sharing this with a wider audience. You aren't asking for any commitment from them. Perhaps you create an online video that begins by pulling the viewer into the future, followed by your insights. You could include an interactive portion as simple as comments, suggestions, or a poll. Anyone with expertise in online training development could help you design this.

If you want to INFLUENCE, you'll craft this for your specific audience. Say you're seeking resources or sponsorship for a critical strategic option you've identified. Again, pull your audience in by describing the future and the threat or opportunity facing your organization. Assemble your data and engage their brain with imagery. As one of our clients told us, "Make it hard for them to say no." And be clear about the ask.

Finally, if you want to INVOLVE another person, function, or stakeholder, you could start with a discussion. Your reputation as someone-who-is-doing-interesting-things may precede you if you've built a good network. Again, be clear about what you're asking for: direct involvement, like joining a steering committee, or becoming part of a launch team, or acting as an expert on loan from another function. Send the link to your cool video in advance and include

"When nothing is certain, anything is possible."

MANDY HALE,
AUTHOR, THE
CHRYSALIS EFFECT

a short briefing document (which may or may not be reviewed in advance). Be ready to share convincing data and evocative images. Convey what a cool opportunity it is to address this threat or opportunity and who's sponsoring it.

No matter what format you select, you'll want to consider HOW you present your insights and recommendations. It's possible to have several versions (short to extensive) depending on your audience. Whatever you chose to create, remember your goals in sharing this work: inform, influence, or involve. And the ultimate goal: to help your organization thrive in the future.

Summary

- Communicate the Case (for action) is about influencing others to act based on the insights and recommendations you've generated.
- Your ultimate goal is to help your organization thrive in the future.
- There are three possible goals for this stage:
  - INFORM: Share important knowledge and insights.
  - INFLUENCE: Make recommendations and obtain sponsorship or budget/commitment/decision.
  - INVOLVE: Engage others in planning and implementation.
- Communicating the case requires images, stories, and data.
- The format and content depend on your audience and their why.

When you've completed this stage, you will have a case for action you can share with a variety of stakeholders. You'll also have a format that tells the story in a way that engages your audience. You've got this!

Your Turn

Take a moment to think about one of your higher-risk scenarios. What do you want to communicate?

_____

_____

_____

_____

_____

_____

_____

_____

Consider one of your key stakeholders. What will they expect from you?

_____

_____

_____

_____

What do you hope will happen?

S10: Integrate and Monitor

In our previous stage, Communicate the Case, you assembled a compelling case for action for key stakeholders. Stage 10 assumes you've been successful in getting engagement and resources for a set of your recommendations. (Way to GO!)

This is where you capitalize on all the work you've completed in your scenario project.

Today for Tomorrow

Although all your focus up to now has been about defining and analyzing the possible futures, this stage is about bringing your insights into today's activities. This stage is about acting. Now is the time to integrate those recommendations into your current business plan.

As a leader, you already know how to do short-term planning, create work plans, and track progress. You have the skills. You're ready to get tactical and execute. These three activities will get you started:
- Orient your team
- Update your current plans
- Identify and monitor signposts

Orient Your Team
It's likely that team members and partners who weren't part of the original scenario work will be involved in the work plans. Perhaps you're bringing in finance colleagues or change management folks. Or maybe you're handing the work off to a project manager. It's important that you bring the new team members up to speed. This is a change effort, and during any change people require four things:

1. *Reason*: Why are we doing this? we recommend sharing the Three Horizons of Growth model (page 19) as part of your story.
2. *Roadmap*: What steps are we taking? Communicate the case to the team. Share the scenarios, insights, and actions.
3. *Role*: What's my part in this? What are the expectations? Describe why they've been tapped to be a part of the team (their strength) and how you'll work together.
4. *Result*: How will we know if we're successful? Create a clear picture of the desired outcome and benefits of that outcome—to each individual and the organization or function.

Update the Current Strategy

At this point, you've assessed the effectiveness of your current strategy to support your organization's health in multiple futures. You've gotten the go-ahead to move forward on a couple of projects.

Here are a few things you can do to amend your current strategy. Think of this exercise as a variation of *Start, Stop, Continue.*

Add Plans
In Stage 8, you identified strategic options and made recommendations on which ones to pursue. Following Stage 9 decisions, these options and recommendations need to become part of your business plan for this year.

Here are the options we recommended for our Future of Supply Chain Case Study. Two of the options only received partial resources, but we know we can identify first steps for each of them:

NO REGRETS – Develop advanced cybersecurity and information defense.
LITTLE BETS – Experiment with alternate locations and sourcing
OPTIONS – Ensure access to power with a Corporate Power Purchase Agreement
LARGE BETS – Collaborate with s*elect partners to create a Resource Trading Ecosystem.*

THE BAADER-MEINHOF PHENOMENON

Baader-Meinhof is a form of selective awareness.

A couple of things happen when it kicks in. One, your brain seems to be excited by the fact that you've learned something new, and selective attention occurs. Your brain subconsciously thinks, "Hey, that's awesome! I'm going to look for that thing without actually thinking about it."

Over twenty years ago Maggie worked with a global team on the future of water. To this day she still notices news about water. Once you become alert to an inquiry you won't 'unsee' it. Your brain will note the data easily.

For each option, you will develop first steps. Little bet experiments will be numerous and of short duration. Your large bet will evolve over several years. The work plan should include a cadence for tracking progress, reviewing results, and harvesting insights.

Prioritize and Eliminate
Because you can't do everything, you may decide to delay or de-fund existing work in your current business plan.

Accelerate Plans
Based on your analysis, you identified several critical uncertainties. Your labor force is aging and robotics is changing desired skill sets in warehousing and manufacturing. You and your colleagues had the skills transition in a 3-year plan but have decided to take proactive steps sooner.

Monitor Signposts

As part of your scenario creation, you identified several critical uncertainties. Look at them again. What might be some indicators that the future is tilting in one direction or another? These early indicators are called signposts. They're trail markers on the path to an evolving future. You will want to define some monitoring routines around them.

In our Future of Supply Chain Case Study, we are tracking multiple signposts based on the uncertainties we identified earlier in our work.

First, we're watching climate law as it emerges. In July 2025 the UN's principal judicial body ruled that Nation States have an obligation to protect the environment from greenhouse gas (GHG) emissions and act with due diligence and cooperation to fulfill this obligation. Several states in the U.S. have been successful in enacting Climate Superfund legislation. We'd like to be early adopters and ensure we're in compliance with global climate law as it emerges.

Our industry relies on consistent and accessible power. We're tracking global innovation in the energy sector for both manufacturing and transport.

We're watching the evolution of technology in manufacturing and transportation. Robotics and drone options make sense in some of our locations.

Finally, we'll continue to monitor the evolving value proposition to key talent and ensure we're optimally staffed as workforce demographics shift.

Build Your Trend Spotting Capability

Anyone can be a trend scanner. Anyone. TrendWatching, a leading consumer trend firm, has a global network of spotters who share what they are seeing in their geographies. Your organization can do the same—formally or informally. It just requires some practices that make the work easy and fun. Here are some ideas to transform your team into a plucky League of Trend Nerds:

- Schedule time to review responsible sources. There's more than you can possibly take in. But over time, you will discover the best of the best.
- Set up browser alerts or an RSS feeder for weak signals or innovations you're tracking.
- Schedule time with a brain trust (ideally, cross-org) and challenge one another to bring the most arcane or novel trends you can find.
- Document. Track. Review for patterns.
- Read and listen widely.
  - Podcasts
  - Trade journals from other domains
  - Off-the-beaten-path magazines
  - International newspapers
- See page 49-51 for a short list of recommended sources.
- Rotate tracking focus using PESTLE—or generate your own version of PESTLE.
- Make trend updates part of a routine.
  - Include them as an agenda item on monthly meetings.
  - Open a channel in your communication system to share trends you're following.
- Have a dorky prize that belongs to that month's winner. The criteria are up to you.

Once you get through this stage, you'll have a work plan to integrate Today for Tomorrow activities and a set of signposts to monitor.

Summary

- This final stage is the payoff for all the work you've done to this point. You're taking action to optimize your organization for the four possible futures.
- There are three key activities in this stage: orient, update, and monitor.
- Orient any team members who were not part of the scenario work. Share the work to date and include the four Rs: reason, roadmap, role, and result.
- Update your current business plan to make scenario actions part of the current business plans.
- Signposts are indicators that the future is emerging in a certain direction. Creating a mechanism to monitor critical uncertainties will avoid the possibility of missing an unanticipated shift.

Your Turn

Pat yourself on the back for your persistence and valor in arriving at this point. Congratulations!

Take a moment to reflect on your journey.

What was most challenging?

_____

_____

_____

_____

_____

What has been energizing?

_____

_____

_____

_____

_____

_____

Describe a couple of your key learnings.

_____

_____

_____

_____

_____

_____

_____

_____

What advice would you give to others as they embark on this journey?

_____

_____

_____

_____

_____

_____

_____

Part Three

Final Words
and Resources

Final Thoughts

That's it. You've completed your introduction to strategic foresight. Congratulations! We wish you all the best in your foresight work. It's been a privilege being on this journey with you.

We will close by saying that we are not passive passengers on the journey to the future. We can do more than react to change—we can anticipate it, prepare for it, and most importantly, we can have a deliberate hand in shaping the outcomes that matter most. Strategic foresight isn't just about predicting what might happen; it's about envisioning the future we actually want to create and taking purposeful steps to bring it into being.

The tools you now possess—scenario planning, trend analysis, and systems thinking—are instruments of agency. They transform you from someone who simply responds to circumstances into someone who actively participates in creating tomorrow's reality. Every scenario you build, every assumption you challenge, every weak signal you identify becomes a building block for more intentional leadership.

As a leader, you now have the capacity to make not just informed choices, but inspired ones. You can see beyond the immediate pressures and quarterly demands to the longer arcs of change that will define your industry, your organization, and the communities you serve. The cumulative effect of these choices—your choices—ripples outward in ways you may never fully see but will undoubtedly feel.

Remember that your influence extends far beyond your official title or organizational chart. As employees, investors, citizens, and consumers, our collective voices and choices create the very future we're trying to anticipate. Every decision you make, every initiative you champion, every conversation you start about what's possible contributes to the great collaborative work of building tomorrow.

We encourage you to use your voice, your vision, and your talent as a leader to work for the world you want to inhabit and leave behind. The future is not something that happens to us—it's something we actively create through the courage of our convictions and the wisdom of our preparation.

You have more power than you know. Now you have the tools to use it wisely.

Further Reading

To learn more about the history of strategic foresight and the process, try:

The Art of the Long View: Planning for the Future in an Uncertain World by Peter Schwartz. This is a classic in the world of scenario planning written by one of the co-founders of the Global Business Network.

Living in the Futures: How Scenario Planning Changed Corporate Strategy by Angela Wilkinson and Roland Kupers. Harvard Business Review, May 2013.

Learning from the Future: How to Make Robust Strategy in Times of Deep Uncertainty by J. Peter Scoblic. Harvard Business Review, July-August 2020.

Effective Data Storytelling: How to Drive Change with Data, Narrative, and Visuals by Brent Dykes.

To explore strategic options, we recommend the following resources:

Rogue Waves: Future-Proof Your Business to Survive and Profit from Radical Change by Jonathan Brill.

Little Bets by Peter Sims.

How to Hedge Your Strategic Bets by Ashish Iyer and George Stalk. Harvard Business Review, May 2016.

Blue Ocean Shift by W. Chan Kim and Renee Mauborgne.

To explore future possibilities through fiction we recommend:

The Ministry of the Future by Kim Stanley Robinson

Klara and the Sun by Kazuo Ishiguro

Project Hail Mary by Andy Weir

Acknowledgements

There's quite a journey from an initial idea—*"You know, there ought to be a how-to book so more leaders can use strategic foresight"*—to the resource now in your hands.

First, we acknowledge the many scenario sages who laid the foundation for this work. Peter Schwartz, Adam Kahane, Paul J.H. Schoemaker, Pierre Wack, Stewart Brand, and others are familiar to us not because we've met them, but because their writing and thinking have guided us for years. We truly stand on the shoulders of giants.

We've been fortunate in our teachers and mentors—your wise words still echo in our minds, shaping how we think and lead. To our many wonderful colleagues: we've learned so much from working alongside you, sharing ideas, wrestling with challenges, and celebrating breakthroughs together. Your insights, questions, and collaborative spirit have enriched our understanding and made us better practitioners. We carry forward the gifts you've given us in every page of this work.

To our clients: thank you for your trust. Each engagement has deepened our practice and understanding. We're especially grateful to the many leaders we've had the privilege to coach and support. Leadership comes in many shapes and styles. Your openness, courage, and commitment continue to inspire us. Your work matters.

Finally, heartfelt gratitude to our people who supported us during the long hours in front of the computer: Susan and Janet; Shane, Mason and Silas. Your support, patience, and encouragement made it all possible. Thank you.

References

Alad, Barry. "Esports Statistics 2025: Market Growth, Viewership, and Trends." *SQ Magazine*, April 21, 2025. https://sqmagazine. co.uk/esports-statistics-2/.

Baghai, Mehrdad, Steve Coley, and David White. *The Alchemy of Growth: Practical Insights for Building the Enduring Enterprise.* New York: Basic Books, 1999.

Berger, Michael. "Autonomous Micro- and Nanobots Capture and Degrade Micro- and Nanoplastics." Nanowerk, 2022. https://www. nanowerk.com/nanotechnology_articles/newsid=59871.php.

Cai, Yanpeng, Zheng Buyun, Lin Xiaofeng, You Xin, Jia Qunpo, and Xue Ni. "Efficient and Stable Extraction of Nano-Sized Plastic Particles Enabled by Bio-Inspired Magnetic 'Robots' in Water." *Environmental Pollution*, 2025.

CGS. "Gen Z Leads Changing Consumer Shopping Habits, Motivations." 2021. https://www.cgsinc.com/blog/gen-z-leads-changing-consumer-shopping-habits-motivations-bc.

Desjardin, Jeff. "How Much Data Is Generated Each Day?" *World Economic Forum*, April 2019. https://www.weforum.org/agenda/2019/04/how-much-data-is-generated-each-day-cf4bddf29f/.

El Mir, Jad, Johnny Yaacoub, and Vincenzo Musumeci. "Passion into Profit: The Future of Esports." Strategy& (part of the PwC network), 2024. https://www.strategyand.pwc.com/m1/en/strategic-foresight/sector-strategies/media/future-of-esports.html.

Future Today Institute. "Foresight Frameworks and Tools." 2022. https://futuretodayinstitute.com/foresight-tools-2/.

REFERENCES

Genetic Engineering & Biotechnology News. "Digital Twin Multi Network Models Could Aid Personalized Therapy, Biomarker, and Drug Discovery." June 2, 2023. https://www.genengnews.com/topics/translational-medicine/digital-twin-tech-could-aid-personalized-therapy-biomarker-and-drug-discovery/.

Granovetter, Mark S. "The Strength of Weak Ties: A Network Theory Revisited." Sociological Theory 1, no. 1 (1983): 201-233.

The Harris Poll. "How Gen Z Shops in 2025: QuestDIY Survey Finds New Trends Shaping Consumer Behavior Today." June 2025. https://theharrispoll.com/briefs/gen-z-shopping-study-findings/.

Hines, Andy, and Jeff Gold. "Professionalizing Foresight: Why Do It, Where It Stands, and What Needs to Be Done." *Journal of Futures Studies* 17, no. 4 (2013): 35-54.

International Federation of Robotics. "TOP 5 Global Robotics Trends 2025." January 22, 2025. https://ifr.org/ifr-press-releases/news/top-5-global-robotics-trends-2025.

Jackson, Carly. "Flag to Free the World." The Seasteading Institute. August 17, 2021. https://www.seasteading.org/flag-to-free-the-world/.

Kahane, Adam. Solving Tough Problems: An Open Way of Talking, Listening, and Creating New Realities. San Francisco: Berrett-Koehler Publishers, 2004.

Kahn, Herman. *On Thermonuclear War.* Princeton: Princeton University Press, 1960.

Kaplan, Jeremy. "Lowe's Prints Comic Books Imagining Sci-Fi Futures — Then Makes Them Real." Digital Trends, 2017. Accessed 2019. https://www.digitaltrends.com/computing/lowes-innovation-lab-comics/.

le Roux, Pieter. "Mont Fleur Scenarios." Global Business Network. https://22172938.fs1.hubspotusercontent-na1.net/hubfs/22172938/The%20Mont%20Fleur%20Scenarios.pdf.

Marinkovic, M., O. Al-Tabbaa, Z. Khan, and J. Wu. "Corporate Foresight: A Systematic Literature Review and Future Research Trajectories." *Journal of Business Research* 144, no. 2 (January 2022): 289-311.

McKinsey & Company. "Diversity Matters Even More: The Case for Holistic Impact." 2023. https://www.mckinsey.com/featured-insights/diversity-and-inclusion/diversity-matters-even-more-the-case-for-holistic-impact.

McKinsey & Company. "The Ten Rules of Growth." 2022. https://www.mckinsey.com/capabilities/strategy-and-corporate-finance/our-insights/the-ten-rules-of-growth.

Ocient. "Beyond Big Data, The Rise of Hyperscale." August 9, 2022. https://ocient.com/tech-papers/beyond-big-data-the-rise-of-hyperscale/.

Patience-Davies, Hari. "The Case of the Missing Author: Just Where Did the Claim That Stories Are 22 Times More Memorable Than Facts Alone Come From?" January 27, 2021. https://patiencedavies.com/2021/01/27/the-case-of-the-missing-author-just-where-did-the-claim-that-stories-are-22-times-more-memorable-than-facts-alone-come-from/.

Ramirez, Rafael, Yasser Bhatti, and Efstathios Tapinos. "Exploring How Experience and Learning Curves Decrease the Time Invested in Scenario Planning Interventions." *Technological Forecasting & Social Change*, 2020. 10.1016/j.techfore.2019.119785.

ReliefRx. Company website. 2025. https://www.relievrx.com/.

Rock, David, and Heidi Grant. "Why Diverse Teams Are Smarter." *Harvard Business Review*, November 2016.

Rohrbeck, René, Cinzia Battistella, and Eelko Huizingh. "Corporate Foresight: An Emerging Field with a Rich Tradition." *Technological Forecasting and Social Change*, 2015. 10.1016/j.techfore.2015.11.002.

Scearce, Diana, Katherine Fulton, and GBN Community. *What If? The Art of Scenario Thinking for Nonprofits*. Global Business Network, 2004.

Schoemaker, Paul J. H., and George S. Day. "How to Make Sense of Weak Signals." *MIT Sloan Management Review* 50, no. 3 (Spring 2009): 81-89.

Shiv, Baba. "Class Takeaways: The Frinky Science of the Human Mind." *Stanford Graduate School of Business Insights*, July 2021. https://www.gsb.stanford.edu/insights/class-takeaways-frinky-science-human-mind.

Sims, Peter. *Little Bets: How Breakthrough Ideas Emerge from Small Discoveries*. New York: Free Press, 2011.

Smith, Kristen. "How Diversity Defeats Groupthink." NeuroLeadership Institute, 2019. https://hub.neuroleadership.com/business-case-how-diversity-defeats-groupthink.

Taylor, Petroc. "Amount of Data Created, Consumed, and Stored 2010-2023, with Forecasts to 2028." Statista, June 30, 2025. https://www.statista.com/statistics/871513/worldwide-data-created/.

Stillman, Daniel. "Minimum Viable Transformation." 2022. https://www.danielstillman.com/blog/minimum-viable-transformation.

The Economist. "Africa's Population Will Double by 2050." March 26, 2020. https://www.economist.com/special-report/2020/03/26/africas-population-will-double-by-2050.

United Nations Population Division. "UN Data." 2022. https://data.un.org/Data.aspx?d=PopDiv&f=variableID%3a67.

Wei, Katherine. "How Many People Do You Need to Change the Culture?" *Sierra*. June, 7, 2018. https://www.sierraclub.org/sierra/how-change-peoples-minds-25-percent-tipping-point.

World Health Organization. "Ageing and Health." Fact sheet, October 2021. https://www.who.int/news-room/fact-sheets/detail/ageing-and-health.

About the Authors

Maggie Kolkena began her professional career as a performer and choreographer (although her father suggested she study bookkeeping). At age forty she decided to pursue a more lucrative profession and was accepted into Pepperdine's prestigious MSOD program where her thesis focused on collaborative creativity, comparing corporate project teams to comedy improv teams.

Facilitation, it turns out, relies on many improvisational skills as well as respected business models. Maggie enjoyed several years as the OD Manager for Intel Labs, where she first learned about strategic foresight and studied with the Global Business Network. She founded Third Thought Consulting in 1995, a small practice focused on leadership development.

The firm has served many clients over 25 years from large systems such as HP, Pacific Power, Johnson & Johnson and Whitbread as well as not-for-profit organizations. Maggie has worked with leaders around the world including China, Bangladesh, the EU, and India. She believes that businesses can and will play a major role in saving our planet for our young people.

Jeana Kats brings a quarter-century of human resources, organizational development, and diversity and inclusion expertise to her leadership and performance coaching practice—most notably from her tenure at Intel Corporation, where she mastered the art of turning corporate complexity into clarity.

Her journey into strategic facilitation began in 2002 when she first observed Maggie's strategic foresight sessions and witnessed what she calls "the magic of making the mystical practical." While Jeana modestly insists she's no strategist herself, leaders consistently seek her out for her rare ability to guide strategic planning processes with both precision and humanity. Her secret weapon? A knack for engaging both analytical rigor and creative intuition, helping teams bridge the gap between data-driven insights and imaginative possibility in their strategic foresight work.

Learn More About This Book

Scan the QR code below to visit our book website for additional resources, updates, and behind-the-scenes content.

www.Today-4-Tomorrow.com

www.ingramcontent.com/pod-product-compliance
Lightning Source LLC
Chambersburg PA
CBHW042346030426

42335CB00031B/3477